Selections From

THE WOMAN
QUESTION
IN EUROPE

A Series of Original Essays

Edited by
Theodore Stanton, M.A.

Selected by
D. G. Rohr
Brown University

MSS Information Corporation
655 Madison Avenue, New York, N.Y. 10021

Library of Congress Cataloging in Publication Data

Rohr, Donald G   comp.
  Selections from The woman question in Europe.

  1. Woman — Social and moral questions — Addresses,
essays, lectures. 2. Women in Europe — Addresses,
essays, lectures. I. Stanton, Theodore, 1851-1925, ed.
The woman question in Europe. II. Title.
HQ1588.R64   301.41'2'094   73-22232
ISBN 0-8422-5158-8
ISBN 0-8422-0387-7 (pbk.)

CONTENTS

PREFACE

Theodore Stanton, editor of *The Woman Question in Europe*, was born in 1851 in Seneca Falls, New York where three years earlier his mother, Elizabeth Cady Stanton, had helped to organize the first woman's rights convention in the United States. After graduation from college he went into journalism and, as Berlin correspondent for the New York *Tribune*, had occasion to meet a number of prominent European feminists who were acquainted with his mother's National Woman's Suffrage Association. From them and their associates he began to collect the reports on the feminist movement in various European countries which he edited and published in 1884.

The selections reprinted here appear uncut but rearranged in sequence. In the original edition Stanton grouped the reports according to ethnic families. So the reports from the "Germanic" countries (Britain, Germany, Austria) preceded those from the Scandinavian, the Latin and the Slavic countries. In this reprinting it seemed useful to have the reports from industrially advanced countries (France and Belgium) precede those from the less advanced (Germany, Austria, Russia).

The authors of the several reports are identified by Stanton in editorial notes which he attached to the text. He was the author of the report on France where he had personal exposure to the laws governing marriage and the status of women when he married a Parisian girl in 1881.

INTRODUCTION.

BY FRANCES POWER COBBE.

[Miss Frances Power Cobbe, daughter of Charles Cobbe, D.L., of New-bridge House, Co. Dublin, was born in 1822, and is the author of the follow-ing works : " An Essay on Intuitive Morals," " Religious Duty," " Broken Lights," " Darwinism in Morals," "The Hopes of the Human Race," " The Duties of Women," " The Peak in Darien," etc. Of late Miss Cobbe has devoted herself almost exclusively to the work of the Victoria Street Society for the Protection of Animals from Vivisection, of which she is the found-ress and Honorary Secretary.]

THERE have been many movements in the world—some of them recorded in history as portentous events, others forgotten within a few years of their occurrence—which may each be compared to a wave on the surface of the Mediterranean. From the insignificant ripple to the wave-high billow flecked with foam and breaking in cataracts, they have arisen only to subside to their original level, leaving the boundaries of land and sea where they have stood for a thousand years. There are other movements, on the contrary, which resemble the tides of the Ocean, wherein each wave obeys one uniform impetus, and car-ries the waters onward and upward along the shore.

Of all the movements, political, social and religious, of past ages there is, I think, not one so unmistakably tide-like in its extension and the uniformity of its impulse, as that which has taken place within living memory among the women of almost every race on the globe. Other agitations, reforms and revolutions have pervaded and lifted up classes, tribes, nations, churches. But this movement has stirred an entire sex, even half the human race. Like the incoming tide, also, it has rolled in separate waves, and each one has obeyed the same law, and has done its part in carrying forward all the rest. The waves of the Higher Education of Women all over the world; the waves which lifted women over the sand-bars of the medical and (in America) of the legal and clerical professions; the waves which seated them on the School Boards and Boards of Guardians of the Poor; the wave which gave them the English Municipal Vote; the wave which restored to Married Women a right to their own property; every one of these waves, great and small, has been rolled forward by the same advancing tide.

But the crown and completion of the progress must be the attainment of the Political Franchise in every country wherein representative government prevails, and till that point be reached, there can be no final satisfaction in any thing which has been achieved. It has been repeated till it has become a commonplace, that " the Suffrage is the key of woman's position." Obtaining it, every privilege she can reasonably desire must follow. Failing to obtain it, nothing,—not even such installments of her rights as she has hitherto enjoyed,—is secure. An easily-raised storm of prejudice and selfishness, whether of trade or party or sect, passing over the masculine population, might sweep away her few privileges, while she remained helpless and unable to protect them by a single vote. On a small scale such confiscations of the rights of women in trades and other matters have occurred again and again. The sufferers had no appeal from injustice, and, because they were unrepresented, their wrongs were overlooked.

The most difficult problem in that great branch of Ethics which we call Politics regards the place which ought to be assigned under each constitutional government to alien races of men. The system of Representation itself, with Trial by Jury and the whole scheme of civil and political liberty, as we, in our day, understand it, has grown up through a thousand years of

> " Freedom slowly broadening down
> From precedent to precedent,"

among our law-abiding Anglo-Saxon race ; and either the hasty adoption of it by other nations with different tendencies and untrained to self-government, or else the sudden admission of aliens in large numbers to a share in the working of our own machinery, are experiments fraught with difficulty and danger. In the Greek, Italian, French and Spanish Chambers we see examples of the first ; and, in the Irish Parliamentary " Obstruction " and misuse of the jury system to defeat justice, of the second. Noble and righteous as was the act by which the government of the United States extended the suffrage to the emancipated negroes, the perils of such a step could scarcely have been encountered by any sane statesman had the lately freed slaves borne a much larger proportion to the whole white population of the Republic ; and not even American democracy will contemplate for many a year to come following up this heroic act by enfranchising Chinese immigrants ; nor English radicalism ask for the admission of Hindoos to a share in the Legislative,— scarcely even in the Executive,—government of India.

Statesmen, even of the broadest views, may not only be pardoned, but praised, for hesitating and taking time for deep consideration, when it is proposed to introduce a new element into the constitution of their country. In my humble judgment, as a Conservative, there has been culpable recklessness on the part of those who, to serve party interests, have, in England, thrown open the gates of our sacred "*polis*" to a rabble of " illiterates," and in America have admitted hordes of immigrants to the ballot-box, before it was possible for them to acquaint themselves with American politics, or to imbibe American principles.

These considerations should induce women, and their generous advocates, to regard without impatience all opposition to their claims to the suffrage which they believe to be honestly intended and grounded on patriotic anxiety lest the introduction of a new force should disturb the working of the machine of State. They should teach them also to frame their arguments with the paramount object of allaying the fears and encouraging the confidence of such worthy opponents, who, when once convinced that the enfranchisement of women will tend to the stability and prosperity of the State, and to the maintenance of social order and religion, will become the most earnest advocates of the measure. The difference—nay, rather the contrast—should likewise be insisted on between proposals to admit the dregs of a population to the franchise, and those to admit the mothers, daughters and sisters of the men who already exercise it ; and again, between proposals to admit aliens of another race, and those to admit women who have the same hereditary tendencies, attachments, creeds and interests ; and who are the inevitable partakers of the nation's prosperity, and the deepest sufferers by its disasters, or misrule. In short, it ought to be the care of the advocates of women to point out that not a single one of the reasons for caution in the case of the admission of aliens affect their claims; while there exist a multitude of valid reasons, why, being by nature part of the nation, they should also be, by law, citizens of the State; bringing with them, not an element of weakness and disintegration, but a completer union, and a contribution to the nation's counsels of something more than " mother-wit," even of mother-wisdom.

The man is not to be envied who can view the struggle of women for political rights with contempt or indifference. That those struggles may not always have been guided by infallible taste and wisdom, and that they have often been met—for lack of sensible argument—with silly derision, need not blind us to the fact that they constitute one of the bravest battles, one of the most pathetic movements, the world has ever seen. Other strifes have been carried on between rival races, rival classes, rival sects; but here we have only the patient, persistent appeal of daughters to fathers; of sisters to brothers; of wives to husbands; of the women, who make the charm of society, to the men who call them friends. There are no " garments rolled in blood " in the battle of these warriors. The combatants command neither cannon nor bayonets. They cannot even break down iron palings, like the populace of London, when the rights they demanded were withheld; or threaten dynamite and petroleum like Nihilists and Fenians. They have not the minutest political influence at their disposal wherewith to coerce their opponents. Never was there a case of such pure and simple Moral Pressure,—of an appeal to justice, to reason, to men's sense of what is due, and right, and expedient for all. When the time comes to look back on the slow, universal awakening of women all over the globe, on their gradual entrance into one privileged profession after another, on the attainment by them of rights of person and property, and, at last, on their admission to the full privileges of citizenship, it will be acknowledged that of all the " Decisive Battles of History," this has been, to the moralist and philosopher, the most interesting ; even as it will be (I cannot doubt) the one followed by the happiest Peace which the world has ever seen.

I feel myself honored in being called on to introduce a worthy and adequate record of this great contest to the public of England and America.

CHAPTER I

FRANCE.

BY THE EDITOR.

CONDORCET, whom Mill, in his "Autobiography," pronounces "one of the wisest and noblest of men," spoke out repeatedly and plainly on the eve of the French Revolution in favor of the rights of women. His "Letters from a Bourgeois of New Haven to a Citizen of Virginia" (*Lettres d'un bourgeois de New Haven à un citoyen de Virginie*), which appeared in 1787, contain an able plea for women's suffrage, and his essay "On the Admission of Women to Citizenship" (*Sur l'admission des femmes au droit de cité**) sounds like an article in the Boston *Woman's Journal* or the London *Englishwoman's Review*. But the great philosopher did not stand alone. Michelet paints a vivid picture of the celebrated orator and member of the Convention, the Abbé Fauchet, speaking in 1790 for women's rights, with Condorcet among his listeners, in the circus, which once stood in the middle of the Palais Royal.† The Abbé Sieyès, Saint Just, and other leaders of the epoch, have left eloquent words in support of women's emancipation.

The press of the Revolution was not silent on the subject. Besides the numerous tracts, pamphlets and even

---

* This essay appeared in the *Journal de la société de 1789*, for July 3, 1790.
† *Les femmes de la révolution*, p. 74.

books which were written for and against the question, several newspapers came out warmly in favor of extended liberty for women. The *Orateur du peuple*, the *Chronique du mois*, which printed articles by Condorcet; the *Bouche de fer*, in which Thomas Paine sometimes wrote; the *Journal de l'état et du citoyen*, the *Cercle social*, and other journals, took up the discussion in a friendly spirit.

But this movement did not spend itself in words alone. The Assembly and the Convention determined to ameliorate the condition of women. The proposed code of the Convention, drawn up by Cambacérès, placed married women on an equality with their husbands, which leads a high legal authority to say, that "such a work of civil legislation was never elaborated in any age or among any people." * In the great question of primary instruction, to cite one more example, the Convention treated alike both boys and girls.

But far more interesting and remarkable is woman's own part in this effort for emancipation. She was no passive spectator.† The "Petition of the Women of the Third Estate to the King" in 1789, is very well written and deals chiefly with the lamentable position of

---

* Emile Acollas, *Le mariage*, p. 98. This is a very able and liberal little book, which presents the whole subject of marriage, both in its legal and moral bearings, in a very instructive and broad-minded manner.

† The historians of the French Revolution have never done full justice to the women of that epoch, sometimes through prejudice and often because of the obscurity which surrounds the subject. As an instance of this latter fact, Michelet (*Les femmes de la révolution*, p. 112) says: "We unfortunately know but little of the history of the women's societies; it is only in the accidental mention of the newspapers, in biographies, etc., that we find some slight traces of them." Lairtuillier (*Les femmes célèbres de la révolution*), has done something toward filling this gap in the literature on the Revolution.

women in the field of work.* Another petition of this same year prays for women's civil and political rights and their admission to the States-General, while still another begs that they be placed on an exact equality with men, and that even the pulpit be opened to them—not a slight request in a Catholic country. The petitioners did not hesitate to solve the most difficult social questions. "Remember that your happiness is absolutely dependent upon that of women," they said to the National Assembly; "the only way perhaps to render it mutually unalterable, is to promulgate a decree obliging men to marry women who have no dower." "The number of these documents makes them more significant and important," says M. Amédée Lefaure, and, I may add on the same authority, they are all the production of women themselves.†

But woman's activity was not confined to petitions. Mlle. d'Orbe, who, as president of one of the women's clubs, pronounced an admirable funeral oration on Mirabeau; the Marchioness of Fontenay (Mme. Tallien), "the woman who saved the city of Bordeaux from massacre,"

---

* Some idea of the industrial position of women prior to the Revolution may be gained from this paragraph by Condorcet (*Sur l'admission des femmes au droit de cité*): " Before the suppression of the *jurandes* [the governing bodies of the old trade corporations] in 1776, women could not acquire the *maîtrise* [the right to the complete exercise of a trade] of a milliner and of other callings, unless married, or unless a man lent or sold them the use of his name, in order that they might obtain the privilege. It is quite singular that a woman could be regent in France, but, until 1776, she might not be a milliner at Paris." Millinery is one of the few occupations which women have latterly gained from men.

† *Le socialisme pendant la révolution.* This book is most liberal in its treatment of the woman question, and contains very curious information concerning the part women played in the upheaval of 1789.

says Legouvé,* "and snatched Paris from the Reign of Terror;" Théroigne de Méricourt, who shouldered the musket in the revolutionary cause;† Rose Lacombe, the leader of the women's clubs; Olympe de Gouges, the author of the "Declaration of the Rights of Women," and of a score of volumes on all sorts of social questions, are a few of the less known names of a long list of women, who in courage, generosity, breadth of mind, extravagance and acts of savagery, even, were unsurpassed by the men of the epoch.

Either singly or in mass, women were the authors of some of the most important episodes of the Revolution. The initiative act of the struggle, the famous petition of the Champ de Mars, which demanded that "neither Louis XVI., nor any other king," should be recognized, was drawn up by a woman, Mme. Robert, *née* Kéralio.‡ In the

---

* *Histoire morale de la femme*, p. 398.

† "The ballot and bullet argument," as it has been called, is often brought forward against women's suffrage. If you vote, you must fight, say the opponents of the enfranchisement of women. The defenders of women's political claims then cite the large number of women who, in all ages and in all countries, have borne arms. An obscure but very striking example of a would-be female warrior recently came to my notice. Mlle. Julie Jussot, of Vergigny, in the department of the Yonne, was placed on the official birth-register under the masculine name, by mistake, of Jules. On reaching twenty-one recently, she received a communication from the mayor of her *commune*, informing her that the moment for military service had arrived. She responded promptly, but on learning her sex, the authorities erased her name from the list of conscripts. In a letter to me, which, by its style and hand-writing, betokens a woman of considerable education, Mlle. Jussot says: "In regard to the conscripts' flag, I demanded permission to carry it, for one's heart ought always to be French, when the defence of one's country is concerned. If the day of revenge comes, although I am not a man, I assure you, sir, that France may count on me to defend her soil." This sentiment has the true ring of a Jeanne Darc.

‡ Michelet, *Les femmes de la révolution*, p. 188.

16

storming of the Bastille and at the *fête* of the Federation, Michelet pronounces women the prime movers. It was their energetic conduct which crowned with success the events of the 5th and 6th of October, 1789, and brought Louis from Versailles to Paris. A French historian has truly said: " Women were the advance-guard of the Revolution." *

Thus the advocacy of great men, and the activity and vigor of women themselves, seemed in the early days of the Revolution to portend the opening of a new era for the female sex. But the authors of the revolt wished only to use the women for the advancement of their own ends. No sooner was the insurrection gotten well under way, than they deserted their worthy coadjutors. In the beginning they encouraged them in the foundation of clubs, and applauded their ardor in the cause, only to abolish these clubs, check this ardor, and finally thrust them back into their old position when the end was gained.† Mirabeau, Danton, Robespierre, *et al.*, soon put a period to this women's movement. The Republic was gradually merged into the Empire, which was the *coup de grâce* of the aspirations of the women of 1789. The Empire not only dissipated their day-dreams, but it fastened the Napoleonic Code about their necks. This was a fatal moment for women's interests. The general public had not forgotten the many disorders in which they had participated, and was unfriendly. The codifiers were dry old followers of the Roman law, and Bonaparte, woman's evil genius, was all powerful. The spirit with which he entered upon the task may be judged by this remark to his

* *Les femmes de la révolution*, p. 24.
† Legouvé, *Histoire morale de la femme*, p. 405.

17

colleagues : " A husband ought to have absolute control over the actions of his wife ; he has the right to say to her : madam, you shall not go out ; madam, you shall not go to the theatre ; madam, you shall not see such or such a person."*

Then came the Restoration and its philosopher, M. de Bonald, who pronounces the *ipse dixit*, "man and woman are not equals, and can never become so." Divorce is abolished, and an attempt is made by the government to re-establish primogeniture.† But this period contained at least one happy event—the birth of the socialistic schools, which, if they have sometimes brought the woman question into bad odor, have also done a great deal to ameliorate the condition of the female sex.‡

---

* Napoleon's misogyny was fully reciprocated. Mme. de Staël's hatred of the Emperor is well known. Ségur, (*Les femmes*), states that the women disliked Napoleon because of his wholesale slaughter of their sons on the field of battle. These mothers had perhaps more ground for their antipathy than the high-strung exile of Coppet. One of the bright spots in this dark period was the appearance in 1801 of Legouvé's " Women's Merit " (*Le mérite des femmes*), a rather heavy poem to-day, but which had a great success at a time when women were without friends at court, and few persons were disposed to sing their praises. Even this poetical defence of women was not allowed to go unanswered. Ménegault published, in this same year, " Men's Merit " (*Le mérite des hommes*), in imitation of Legouvé's poem, and as a set-off to it.

† This would have been a tremendous blow to women, for, as will be seen further on in this chapter, the French law of inheritance places daughters on an absolutely equal footing with sons, one of the very few provisions of the Napoleonic Code which treats women with the same justice as men.

‡ An old Saint Simonian, one of the dozen still alive, M. Charles Lemonnier, once told me that it was due to the efforts of his sect that women are employed by the railroad companies as guards at the highway crossings. The first railroad in France, that between Paris and St. Germain, which was inaugurated in the early days of Louis Philippe's reign, introduced this custom,

With the liberal re-awakening of 1830, the woman question again came to the front. The socialists, individual women, societies, and newspapers, began to take up the subject. Among the women's rights journals were *La femme nouvelle*, which appeared from 1832 to 1834, and the *Gazette des femmes*, which was published from 1836 to 1838, under the editorship of Mme. Poutret de Mauchamps. She based her agitation on the *Charte* or Constitution of 1830, and took the position that, in proclaiming the political emancipation of Frenchmen, the generic term was used, so that the new charter of liberties necessarily included Frenchwomen in its provisions.*

Mme. de Mauchamps appears to have understood the importance of attaching some well-known personages to her agitation. One of the articles is headed, "Men, Worthy of the Name, who Demand the Civil and Political Rights of Women." Then follows a list of some Parisian celebrities, and among others, Jules Janin, the distinguished critic of the *Journal des débats*, and Châteaubriand. The readers of the *Gazette* are informed that the latter " has called and said to us, ' Count me among your subscribers ; you defend a grand and noble cause. ' " Jules Janin contributes at least one article to the paper, a fine estimate of George Sand ; and Charles Nodier, the

---

and I never see one of these sturdy women, as the train whizzes by, a baton at her shoulder, without thinking that the eccentric Saint Simon accomplished some practical good in the world.

* Mme. de Mauchamps held that *les français*, as employed in the *Charte*, embraced *les françaises*, and that *tous, chacun*, etc., wherever they occur in that document, refer to women as well as to men. She therefore addressed a petition to the King, with the following heading : " Petition of Frenchwomen to Louis Philippe I., praying that he declare, in virtue of the Charter of 1830, that he is King of Frenchwomen as he is King of Frenchmen " (*qu'il est roi des françaises comme il est roi des français*).

prolific author and member of the Academy, writes a short book review in one of the numbers.*

Every issue of the *Gazette des femmes* begins with a petition to the King and Parliament, praying for reforms in the Code, for political rights, for the admission of women to the Institute,† etc. In the number for January, 1838, a demand was made that women be admitted to the universities and given degrees. It was forty years before France would listen to this petition, and what was askèd under the Orleans monarchy is only just beginning to be granted under the Third Republic. And yet these petitions, ably drawn up, and sensible in their claims, several times reported and briefly discussed, were heaped with ridicule in the Chamber and quickly forgotten.

That this movement had attracted a share of public attention is evidenced in many ways. The *Gazette* informs us that at one of the elections several voters, instead of casting their ballots for the candidate, gave them to his wife, as a protest against the exclusion of women from the franchise. Mme. Hortense Allart de Méritens, the novelist and historian, writes to the editor of the approaching foundation of an "Association for the Amelioration of Women's Condition," but I find no further mention of this

---

* Nodier could not have been under the influence of Mme. de Mauchamps when he penned for *Le dictionnaire de la conversation* his paper entitled *La femme libre.*

† Alexandre Dumas said in the French Academy a short time ago: "We frequently, and very justly, invoke the authority of Mme. de Sévigné and Mme. de Staël, and yet, if these two celebrated women were alive to-day, we would not give them a seat in our midst. We have, perhaps, been sometimes struck by this contradiction, by this injustice, and we must have said to ourselves: 'As woman can be man's equal in virtue and intelligence, why may she not also be his equal in society, in our institutions, and before the law?'"—Report on the Botta Prize, sitting of May 10, 1881.

organization. In September, 1834, appeared the *Amazone*. The National Library contains only the prospectus of this paper, which was to be a daily for " the political education of women," and which was to treat the question in a serio-comic vein.* The agitation attracted the attention of Mme. de Girardin, who refers to it several times in her brilliant " Parisian Letters " (*Lettres Parisiennes*).

Laboulaye's " Inquiries concerning the Civil and Political Condition of Women from the Times of the Romans to the Present " (*Recherches sur la condition civile et politique des femmes depuis les Romains jusqu'à nos jours*), and Legouvé's " Moral History of Woman " (*Histoire morale de la femme* †), both appeared during the reign of Louis Philippe, and did a great deal to direct the public mind to the lamentable condition of women before the law. M. Legouvé's book, conceived in a very liberal spirit, and written in a charming style, was soon read all over Europe. " Equality in difference " ("*l'égalité dans la différence*") is its key-note. " The question is not to make woman a man, but to complete man by woman," says the author in another part of the volume.

While this Platonic consideration of the woman question was in progress, the Revolution of February suddenly burst upon France, and for a moment it seemed as if the

---

* Its epigraph was as follows :

> *Les hommes ne sont pas ce qu'un vain sexe pense,*
> *Ils sont trop étourdis pour gouverner la France.*

† Although this work was published after the advent of the Revolution of February, its contents had been delivered as a series of lectures at the College of France during the last year of the July monarchy. M. Legouvé is the son of the author of *Le mérite des femmes*, to which poem reference has already been made, and, for a Frenchman, holds very advanced ideas on the woman question.

era of the actual emancipation of women had come at last. But the magnificent dreams of the Second Republic were, in so far as concerned women, never realized. " In 1848 there was a grand agitation," Laboulaye once wrote me, " great demands, but I know of nothing durable or solid on this question." " The intrigues and fatal days of June, 1848, and June, 1849, absorbed public attention," Jeanne Deroin Desroches* writes me ; " men of influence took little interest in social questions, and especially that of the emancipation of women. We were finally prohibited from having anything to do with the political clubs,† and the police aided in the getting up of meetings and societies of women, such as that of the *Vésuviennes*, composed of prostitutes, which burlesqued everything we said and did, in order to cast ridicule and contempt on our meetings and our acts." In a word, the movement of 1848—and there was a great movement at this epoch—was swallowed up in Socialism. and Socialism destroyed itself by its own extravagance.

But the women had some staunch friends at this time. Victor Considérant, the well-known disciple of Fourier, was "the only one of the nine hundred members of the Con-

---

* Mme. Desroches, one of the enthusiasts and martyrs of this period, is now living at an advanced age, at Shepherd's Bush, near London.

† It was a Protestant Minister, Athanase Coquerel, the most distinguished member of the celebrated family of clergymen, the Beecher family of France, who laid before the Chamber the bill for the exclusion of women from the clubs. He was very roughly handled for this act by several feminine pens. See *Almanach des femmes* for 1852. This curious little publication, in French and English, was due to the indefatigable Jeanne Deroin. The first number, which appeared at Paris in 1852, was seized by the police, and the subsequent numbers, those for 1853 and 1854, were issued at London. These modest little annuals throw a flood of light on a very confused period.

stituent," writes Jeanne Deroin, "who demanded women's political rights in the Committee on the Constitution." When, in the summer of 1851, it was proposed in the Chamber to deny women the right of petition in political affairs, M. Laurent, of the Department of the Ardèche, M. Schœlcher, the celebrated Abolitionist, the Garrison of France, and M. Crémieux, opposed the proposition, and it-was defeated.* When the subject of the reorganization of the communes came up, in November, 1851, M. Pierre Leroux, the famous Socialistic Radical, offered an amendment to the first article of the bill, to the effect that "the body of electors be composed of French men and women of legal age." He supported his amendment in a speech which filled three columns of the official newspaper, and which was received by the Chamber with shouts of laughter.†

The Revolution of 1848 was as fecund in newspapers as it was in socialistic Utopias. Among the former were many women's journals. I have run over some of these and found them highly interesting, often amusing, but always sincere and earnest. *La politique des femmes*, "published in the interest of women by a society of working women," as we are informed, and which became, later, *L'opinion des femmes*, and *La voix des femmes*, edited by Mme. Eugénie Niboyet, a woman of considerable literary talent who died in 1882, are, perhaps, two of the best specimens of these women's rights' papers.

The French propensity to turn everything to ridicule— and there was, indeed, much material for its gratification at this time—found an outlet in *La république des femmes*, "the journal of the petticoats" (*cotillons*) as its

---

* See the *Moniteur*, June 24 and July 3, 1851.
† Id., November 22, 1851.

sub-title reads, which appeared in June, 1848, and poked fun at the women who participated in the public life of the day.

In April, 1851, M. Chapot proposed in the Legislative Assembly to restrain the right of petition in the case of men, and to suppress it entirely for women in all matters of a political nature. Jeanne Deroin, confined at St. Lazare as a political prisoner, issued a vigorous protest from her cell. M. Laurent presented this petition and attacked the Chapot resolution. A debate ensued, and the question was adjourned to July 2d. On that date M. Schœlcher, who is to-day a member of the Senate, offered an amendment protecting women's right of petition. M. Crémieux, who was later a member of the Government of National Defence, seconded the amendment, which was finally adopted. The Chapot resolution was then unanimously rejected.

But the Republic fell, and the Second Empire rose on its ruins. The women's movement was abruptly checked. In 1858 Proudhon published " Justice in the Church and in the Revolution " (*La justice dans l'église et dans la révolution*), in which occurs an extended sociologic study of woman. He favors the androgynous couple as the social unit, without, however, attributing an equivalent value to the two parties who constitute it. Man, he says, is to woman in the proportion of three to two. The inferiority of the latter is, consequently, according to Proudhon, irremediable. Newspaper articles, pamphlets and books, attacking this volume, appeared in large numbers, and among them, Mme. Jenny P. d'Héricourt's " The Enfranchised Woman," (*La femme affranchie*), and Mme. Juliette Lambery's (Mme. Adam) " Anti-Proudhonian Ideas on Love, Woman, and Marriage " (*Idées antiproud-*

honiennes sur l'amour, la femme et le mariage), which Professor Acollas pronounces "the most eloquent and the most peremptory refutation of the absurd opinions of P. J. Proudhon on woman." *

The writings of Michelet, Jules Simon, Emile de Girardin, Eugène Pelletan, Leroy-Beaulieu, Emile Deschanel, Mlle. Julie Daubié, and many others, touching upon different phases of the woman question, belong to this or a little later period. Michelet, in his "Woman" (*La femme*) and "Love" (*L'amour*), establishes his famous theory of the "sick woman" (*la femme malade*); Jules Simon, in his "Working Woman" (*L'ouvrière*); Leroy-Beaulieu, in his "Women's Work in the Nineteenth Century" (*Le travail des femmes au dixneuvième siècle*); and Mlle. Daubié, in "The Poor Woman of the Nineteenth Century" (*La femme pauvre au dixneuvième siècle*), show up the lamentable industrial position of women; Emile de Girardin calls attention to the condition of woman in the family; while Eugène Pelletan, in his volume entitled "The Mother" (*La mère*), demands the suffrage for women.† The opinions of these thoughtful and liberal-minded writers had a powerful influence on French public opinion, and prepared the way for those reforms in favor of women, some of which have already occurred, and others of which must follow in the near future, unless the reactionary party once more gets the upper hand.

---

* *Le mariage*, p. 35, note.

† "By keeping woman outside of politics, we diminish by one-half the soul of the country."—*La mère*, p. 233. The late M. Rodière, the distinguished Professor of the Toulouse Law School, in his "Great Jurisconsults" (*Les grands jurisconsultes*), published in 1874, is outspoken in favor of women's suffrage. See pp. 509–512. His language is the more remarkable from the fact that he was a strict Catholic, and, at the same time, a republican, a very rare combination in the France of to-day.

The women's movement took on a more organized form during the last years of the Empire, and M. Léon Richer grouped about himself and his paper, *L'avenir des femmes*, which still exists as *Le droit des femmes*, the more active friends of the question, and succeeded in securing the support of many distinguished writers and statesmen.

Under the Third Republic the woman question, like every other liberal measure, has gained new life and vigor. At the beginning of 1871, Mlle. Julie Daubié, "one of the worthiest women I have ever known," says Laboulaye, announced in the public prints the approaching organization of an Association for Women's Suffrage, but died before accomplishing her object.*

In 1874, at the time of the discussion of the new electoral law in the Versailles Assembly, M. Raudot, of the Right, proposed that every married elector or widower with a child should have two votes. Another deputy, M. de Belcastel, was in favor of the same proportion, but would give the widower two votes whether he had children or not. The Count de Douhet went still further: he would give every man, first a vote for himself, another for his wife, and finally one for each child. The committee to which these projects were referred accepted the principle, and article seventh of the bill which they reported read as follows: "Every married elector, or widower with children or grandchildren, shall have a double vote." Although this article was rejected, it shows that there are men in France who think that women and the family are not sufficiently represented under the present electoral system.

---

* "Mlle. Daubié," Mme. Griess-Traut writes me, "was the first female bachelor of arts in France. She encountered great difficulty in obtaining her diploma, but succeeded in 1862, I think."

In the summer of 1878 occurred at Paris the first International Women's Rights Congress, due in large part to the exertions of M. Léon Richer. The Organizing Committee contained representatives from six different countries, viz.: France, Switzerland, Italy, Holland, Russia, and America. Among the eighteen members from Paris were two senators, five deputies, and three Paris municipal councilors. Italy was represented by a deputy and the late Countess of Travers. The American members were Julia Ward Howe, Mary A. Livermore, and Theodore Stanton. Among the members of the Congress, besides those just mentioned, were Colonel T. W. Higginson, and deputies, senators, publicists, journalists, and men and women of letters from all parts of Europe. The work of the Congress was divided into five sections, as follows: the historical, the educational, the economic, the moral, and the legislative. The proceedings of these different sections have been published in a volume, which forms a valuable collection of the most recent European and American thought on the various phases of the woman question. *

About this time was founded the Society for the Amelioration of the Condition of Women, of which Mlle. Maria Deraismes and Mme. Griess-Traut are the moving spirits. In 1876 Mlle. Hubertine Auclert, radical, earnest, indefatigable, established a Woman's Rights Society, whose special aim is to secure the suffrage for women, and in February, 1881, appeared the first number of its uncompromising organ, *La citoyenne*. Mme. Koppe, who though poor in purse is rich in purpose, published at Paris, from 1880 to 1882, *La femme dans la famille et la société*, a

* *Actes du congrès international des droits des femmes* ; Paris : Ghio, Palais-Royal.

little journal which advocated bravely every good reform. In the autumn of 1882 two new women's rights associations were organized. M. Léon Richer created the French Women's Rights League, whose principal object is to improve the legal condition of French women, and Mlle. Hubertine Auclert converted her Women's Rights Society into a National Women's Suffrage Society, whose aims are sufficiently indicated by its name. During the past few years, mainly through Mlle. Auclert's efforts, meetings have been held and petitions signed in favor of women's suffrage both at Paris and in the provinces. But the reformers have encountered great opposition. Here is one remarkable example of this selected from a large number. M. de Goulard, Minister of the Interior in 1873, refused to allow Mme. Olympe Audouard, whose voice and pen have always been devoted to the interests of her sex, to speak at Paris on the woman question " for three reasons." Here are two of them : " 1. These lectures are only a pretext to bring together a body of women already too emancipated. 2. The theories of Mme. Olympe Audouard on the emancipation of women are subversive, dangerous, immoral." *

We have now glanced rapidly at the principal features

---

* Besides the books already mentioned in the course of the preceding pages, I give here, for the reader who may wish to examine more thoroughly this interesting subject, the titles of two short volumes written in a friendly spirit, and treating the question in a general manner. *La femme libre*, by M. Léon Richer; Paris : E. Dentu, Palais-Royal. *Essai sur la condition des femmes en Europe et en Amérique*, by M. Léon Giraud ; Paris : Auguste Ghio, Palais-Royal. M. Richer's *L'avenir des femmes* (Paris, 4 rue des Deux Gares), a monthly publication, and Mlle. Hubertine Auclert's *La citoyenne* (Paris, 12 rue Cail), also a monthly, give a good idea of current opinion in France on the woman question.

of the more radical phase of the women's movement in France since 1789 up to the present day. I shall next consider the actual situation, treating it under separate heads, as follows: 1. Laws; 2. Morals; 3. Religion; 4. Charity; 5. Instruction; 6. Literature; 7. Fine Arts; 8. Industry; 9. Socialism.

"The Revolution, as has already been seen, signally failed," writes M. Léon Giraud,* "in all that concerned woman. Especially in establishing her legal status did it deviate widely from its principles. This was due in no small degree to the writings of Rousseau. In his *Émile*, Rousseau discusses the theory of woman considered as a child, and adopts the principle of virile and non-virile functions which constituted the basis of ancient Roman law, but which the jurisconsults of the second and third centuries of our era had already begun to repudiate.† Curiously

---

* M. Léon Giraud, *docteur-en-droit*, is a graduate of the Paris Law School. His legal studies early convinced him of the necessity of a complete revision of the laws affecting the family. He gave himself wholly up to this subject, and sought, in travels in foreign countries, the justification of his own theories. His work on the "Condition of Woman in Europe and America" (*Essai sur la condition de la femme en Europe et en Amérique*) was sent to the French Academy in 1883, in competition for the Botta prize, and gave rise to a warm discussion in that learned body. In this synthesis of the woman question, the author comes out in favor of female suffrage. Hence the originality of the book and the cause of its ill-success at the Academy. An earlier volume, bearing the rather odd title, the "Romance of the Christian Woman" (*Le roman de la femme chrétienne*), was historical in its nature, and considered from an entirely new point of view the subject of the conversion of woman to Christianity. Various pamphlets and articles for periodicals preceded these publications. Among the former may be mentioned "Souvenirs of the Women's Rights Congress" (*Souvenirs du congrès pour le droit des femmes*), written apropos of the first International Women's Rights Congress, held at Paris in 1878.

† Gaius's "Institutes," Book I., § 190.—L. G.

29

enough Portalis's preliminary considerations on marriage in the introduction to the Napoleonic code, are taken in large part almost *verbatim* from *Émile*.* Never, in a word, was the idea of justice to women more foreign to any code of laws than to that of 1804.

"Let us first consider married women. In the new code, as in the old, they lose independence and become incapable of ownership, with all its rights and privileges. Of the different matrimonial systems placed by the code at the disposition of the contracting parties, none guarantees woman's liberty. Under none may the wife act, in regard to her property, with the same freedom as the most ignorant man. In one case—the system of 'community of goods' (*communauté de biens*)—she is treated as if weak-minded and in need of a committee; in another—the system by which each spouse is left the separate owner of his or her property (*séparation de biens*)—she is looked upon as a prodigal requiring a guardian. These variations of the old idea, that the wife should be in subordination, are based on principles borrowed from the common law (*coutumes*) of the sixteenth century, and, in certain cases, are even severer on women than the prescriptions of three hundred years ago.

"It is true that the civil code says, with odd *naïveté* or singular assurance, that the matrimonial systems which it presents are only illustrations, limiting in no respect the liberty of the contracting parties.† But do not believe it. This pretended liberty is defined by the article which im-

---

* Compare Fenet's " Preliminary Reports " (*Travaux préparatoires*), Vol. IX., pp. 177 *et seq.*, and all the first part of the fifth book of *Émile*.—L. G.

† The law does not regulate the conjugal union, as regards property, except in default of special conventions which the spouses may make as they see fit. * * * —Civil Code, Art. 1387.

mediately follows, and which informs us that there is a marital authority, a husband who is the head of the family in this new code as in the old.* And several other articles occur farther on in the code, thrice repeating the wife's subordination, stating what deprivations public order and morality require of her, and especially divesting her of that right *par excellence* of ownership, the alienation and free disposition of her property.† It may be understood from this what is meant, when woman is concerned, by those 'imprescriptible' and 'inalienable' rights which were the motto of the Revolution; they are the rights which the husband has over the wife! This statement must be read twice before it can be believed. But the tenor of our law, which nobody questions, and the constant practice of eighty years, leave us no room for doubt.

" The right of alienation, which is an inherent attribute of ownership, and which, according to the economic principles of 1789, was so inseparable from the idea of property that the one could not be understood without the other—even mortmain having been abolished for the simple reason of its restrictive character—this right is a myth in so far as it relates to woman. And yet this same woman

---

* The spouses may annul neither the rights resulting from the marital authority over the person of the wife and children, nor those pertaining to the husband as head of the family. * * * —Civil Code, Art. 1388.

† * * * she [the wife separated from her husband] may not alienate her real estate without the husband's consent. * * * —Civil Code, Art. 1449. The husband retains the control of the real and personal property of the wife, and, consequently, the right to the revenues derived from her dower or from property coming to her during the marriage. * * * —*Id.*, Art. 1538. * * * she [the wife] may not alienate them [paraphernalia] or go to law concerning them, without the husband's consent. * * * —*Id.*, Art. 1576.

was solemnly declared, by the reform of the laws of succession, capable of absolute ownership and of a personal and exclusive title to public riches. The daughter who, as Pothier informs us, was formerly passed over 'in favor of the sons as regards the greater part if not all of the estate, inherits equally with the male children according to the code of 1804, as was also the case in 1792. Neither distinction of sex nor primogeniture is recognized in our present laws of descent.* The daughter, who once counted as a fraction or a zero, is now an integer. This reform has become a permanent part of our legislation. When in 1826, under the Restoration, a bill was laid before parliament for the re-establishment of primogeniture, the effort broke down completely. But once married, this same woman ceases to be an owner in the true signification of the word. Either our law of inheritance is nonsense or our marriage system an error. We must accept one or the other conclusion. Our legislators cannot consistently pronounce such contradictions in one and the same breath, without displaying an absence of philosophy and logic, to be explained only on the ground of complete indifference to the best interests of woman.

" If we now consider the more intimate relations existing between husband and wife and the authority of parents over children, we find that the dominant idea which inspires this portion of our code has also been handed down from the sixteenth century.

"Conjugal fidelity is declared reciprocal in a singularly untruthful article,† and yet the husband and wife are in

---

* The children or their heirs inherit * * * without distinction of sex or birth.—Civil Code, Art. 745.

† The spouses owe each other mutual fidelity, succor and assistance.— Civil Code, Art. 212.

no respects treated alike. The latter is held strictly to account for any moral laxity, under penalty of separation,* and even of several years' imprisonment,† while the former has only to guard against one thing—the law declares it formally—persistent concubinage.‡ It is in fact polygamy which the law condemns. But the definition of marriage would have been sufficient to prohibit this. The wife, therefore, must submit to every license on the part of her husband until this extreme is reached, and even then he is only slightly fined.§

" The father alone, as long as he lives, enjoys authority over the children.‖ He has custody over them, he may punish them, he superintends their education ; when they would marry, it is his consent which must be obtained.¶

---

* The husband may demand a divorce on account of his wife's adultery.— Civil Code, Art. 229.

† The wife convicted of adultery shall be punished with imprisonment for at least three months and not more than two years.—Penal Code, Art. 337.

‡ The wife may demand a divorce on account of her husband's adultery when he shall have kept his concubine under the common roof.—Civil Code, Art. 230. The first and last of the three foregoing articles are no longer in force on account of the abolition of divorce, but they are given as showing the spirit of the code.

§ The husband who shall have kept a concubine under the common roof, and who shall have been convicted thereof on the complaint of the wife, shall be punished by a fine from one hundred to two thousand francs.— Penal Code, Art. 339.

‖ The child, at whatever age, should honor and respect his father and mother.—Civil Code, Art. 371. He is subject to their authority until his majority or emancipation.—*Id.*, Art. 372. The father alone exercises this authority during marriage.—*Id.*, Art. 373. The last article destroys the force of the first two,—one of the many absurd contradictions of this much-vaunted French code.

¶ The son under twenty-five and the daughter under twenty-one may not marry without the consent of their father and mother ; in case of disagreement, the consent of the father suffices.—Civil Code, Art. 148. Could anything be more nonsensical than such an article as this ?

The mother is regarded legally as if she did not exist. When she becomes a widow, her inferiority is further emphasized, for she is still kept under a sort of marital power which discredits her in the eyes of her children. This situation is not justified on the specious pretext of the necessity of there being a head as between two rivals, and its character is the more humiliating for this very reason. The widow is indeed made the legal guardian of her children, but her husband on dying may impose upon her an adviser, without whose consent she cannot exercise the duties of guardianship,—which amounts to taking away with one hand what is given with the other.* It is scarcely necessary to say, that the dying mother possesses no such prerogatives in respect to the widower. Again, the widow who marries may see the guardianship of her children pass completely from her control to that of a custodian, named by a family council.† Furthermore, the power of sending children to prison undergoes a singular modification when transferred from the father to the mother, becoming less energetic in her hands.‡

"Such are the principal features of woman's position in the family. But she has other disabilities than those already mentioned. For example, she may not be a guardian nor a member of a family council, except in the ascending line, as mothers and grandmothers; she may not be a witness to any legal document, nor the publisher of a political newspaper; she may not call a public meeting.§ Nor is this all, but from these facts we readily per-

---

* Civil Code, Art. 391.
† Civil Code, Art. 395.
‡ Compare Civil Code, Arts. 376 and 381.
§ This list might be made much larger. But, more important than the number of these disabilities, is the unwillingness shown by French legis

ceive what is the legal status of woman in France, and are able to judge whether the wife and mother, in the narrow sphere to which she has been relegated, enjoys the influence and rank which she merits.

"We now take up the grave question of the young girl. And this brings us face to face with the important subject of affiliation (*la recherche de la paternité*). According to our code every child born outside of wedlock is considered to be fatherless,* unless, of his own free will, the father formally acknowledges his offspring. Statistics show what a poor resource this is for the bastard: it occurs but once in fifty times.† In no case, except rape, which is almost unknown in France, can the father of an illegitimate child be prosecuted. He is under no obligations to the child any more than to the mother. A promise of marriage, even when made in writing, counts for nothing. A cohabitation extending over many years, even a whole life-time, creates, in the eyes of the law, no presumption against the man. The same thing is true of any private papers containing reiterated avowal of

lators to remove any of them. One instance of this is worth citing: In the month of March, 1881, M. de Gasté introduced into the Chamber of Deputies a bill making women electors for the tribunals of commerce, which decide many of the differences arising between tradesmen. The bill did not pass, and, Gambetta, who was then Speaker, seized the occasion to perpetrate a witticism at the expense of the women. It should be remembered that in no country of the world are there so many women occupying important and independent positions in trade, as in France.

* Affiliation is forbidden. * * * —Civil Code, Art. 340.

† For valuable details on this subject of affiliation, see the remarkable report of Senators Schœlcher, de Belcastel, Foucher de Careil and Bérenger, which was printed in the *Journal Officiel* of May 15, 1878. See also the bill of M. de Lacretelle on the re-establishment of turning-boxes (*tours*) introduced the same year. It may be added that the Senate took no action on either of these propositions.—L. G.

paternity and of measures taken, either at birth or later, for the maintenance and support of the child.* A man may employ every means in his power, short of brute force, to seduce a girl, but no reparation can be obtained. Such is the harsh doctrine of our law. The truth of this statement cannot be questioned. The text of the code, the preparatory reports and the practice of our courts, all agree in this interpretation. Since the promulgation of the Napoleonic code, four score years ago, you cannot find in the whole history of French jurisprudence one single case of a man forced to acknowledge his child. Our ancient jurisprudence contained this maxim : 'The author of the child must support it' ('*qui a fait l'enfant doit le nourrir*').† What a change from one epoch to another ! It could not be more complete.‡

---

* The proposition of M. Demolombe, one of our first jurisconsults, to make affiliation depend on the treatment of the child as one's own (*possession d'état*), met with no favor. See Demolombe's Commentaries on Arts. 319 *et seq.*—L. G.

† Loysel's " Institutes of Common Law " (*Institutes coutumières*).— L. G.

‡ One example selected from thousands may be given to prove, that not only are the statements of the text not exaggerated, but that they are even too mild. M. Alexandre Dumas has just published a powerful arraignment of the French code in its treatment of affiliation. The pamphlet was called forth by a recent decision of the French Court of Appeals. Mlle. G—— became a domestic in the house of M. G——, a farmer and married relative much older than herself. They became intimate and two children were born. Mlle. G—— found a place at Paris, when M. G—— ceased to aid her. Thereupon her guardian sued for damages, basing his claim on seduction, the youth of Mlle. G——, and the fact that her seducer was her relative and should have been her protector. The provincial court, where the case was tried, condemned M. G—— to pay 6,000 francs. He appealed, and the Paris Court of Appeals decided on June 28, 1883, that the seduction had not been accomplished by actionable means, and that M. G—— was responsible only before "the tribunal of his own conscience." It reversed

"And does the State, since it does not hold the father responsible for his illegitimate children, do anything to supply his place? At the beginning of the century, and almost up to the second half, the country undertook on a large scale the care of foundlings, by the establishment of turning-boxes (*tours*), which allowed the unfortunate mother to deposit secretly, and without being subjected to any formalities, her child in the hands of those who would care for it. But, strange to say, at the moment when the turning-boxes were the most necessary on account of the increasing number of abandoned infants, they were gradually suppressed (from 1840 to 1860). In a word, the State in its turn forsook the children and broke the solemn promise, given the mothers of France in 1811, to repair in part the great injustice done them, when it relieved the fathers of all the duties of paternity. Abortion and infanticide consequently increased, until they have reached such a point that the juries, weary of punishing without producing any effect, now often simply acquit the culprit. Such is the present situation : the seducer responsible neither to the child nor its mother; the latter, if poor, reduced to infanticide or prostitution.

"And what does the code do to protect the girl? Almost nothing. While it affords man every facility for the gratification of his passions, it shows an indifference for woman to be found probably in no other system of laws. We guard the girl up to the age of thirteen, but

---

the decision of the lower court, and ordered the poor girl not only to return the 6,000 francs, but to pay costs. Such inhumanity seems almost impossible at Paris, "the capital of civilization," and in the last quarter of the nineteenth century. And yet the creation of this abominable code is considered one of the greatest of Napoleon's honors.

beyond that year she must look out for herself.* The code does not shield her, but rather shields the man. From 1832 to 1863, in which year the law was put on the statute book, the young girl was protected only until the age of eleven, and previous to 1832, girls of the tenderest years might be defiled, provided violence was not used.† Is not the source to be found here of many of the cancerous evils which are fast eating out the life of our social system?

"Is woman sufficiently protected when, according to our penal code and the firmly-established practice of our courts,.the inciting of minors to debauch, even when systematic and long-continued, is not punishable, provided the debaucher is seeking to gratify his own passions and is not acting the part of a pander?‡ Is she sufficiently protected when the father, who has made a traffic of his daughter's virtue, does not thereby lose paternal authority over the other children, who still remain subject to his exclusive and dishonorable control?§ Is she sufficiently protected when the husband's adultery is permitted up to a point where it becomes almost complete impunity? Is she sufficiently protected when our system of legalized prostitution owes its very existence to the con-

---

* Any outrage on decency consummated or attempted without violence on the person of a child of either sex under thirteen years of age, shall be punished with imprisonment * * * —Penal Code, Art. 331.

† See commentary on Arts. 331 and 332 of the Penal Code.

‡ Whoever outrages public morals by habitually inciting, aiding or abetting the debauchery or corruption of the youth of either sex under twenty-one years of age, shall be punished * * * —Penal Code, Art. 334. The commentary on this article reads : "Art. 334 is inapplicable to him who, in inciting minors to debauch, is acting for himself and not for others." Three decisions of the Supreme Court, supporting this view, are given.

§ Compare Penal Code, Art. 335, second paragraph, and Civil Code, Book I., Title IX.

stant, unpunished practice of inciting minors to debauch ? *
No; it is too evident that so long as the Napoleonic
code thus forgets almost every one of the material and
moral interests of woman, so long will it hang as a mill-
stone about the neck of our France, so bravely struggling for her political regeneration.

"The divorce question now occupies a great deal of the
public attention of this country, and is very closely connected with the existing system of partial divorce or the
separation of a married woman from the bed and board
of her husband (*séparation de corps*). One of the chief
reasons given for the re-establishment of divorce, which,
introduced by the Revolution, existed until 1815, is the
effect it will have on this class of women. We have
already seen that the wife's separation from the husband
does not free her from marital power, even when she is
the applicant, which is the case nine times out of ten.
She continues to bear his name, and sees her fortune still
subject in a measure to his control, so that the husband,
if he would take revenge for an adverse judgment, finds
here an excellent opportunity to hector his former wife.
Although our publicists, both those for and against
divorce, have spoken out in opposition to this state of
things, no change has been made.

"Another anomaly of this partial divorce was suppressed, but in favor of the husband, it must be said. I
refer to the presumption that the husband was the father
of any children born after the separation, even when all
cohabitation had ceased.† Since 1850, however, the husband has only to confront the date of the child's birth

---

* See Yves Guyot's " Prostitution " (*La prostitution*).—L. G.
† The old maxim put it : *Pater is est quem nuptiæ demonstrant.*—L. G.

39

with the date of the separation, to prove that he is not its father.   This reform is perfectly just, but it is a curious fact that our law-makers introduce innovations only when their own sex is to be benefited thereby.

" What would be the situation of the divorced wife if, without any other changes in the code, M. Naquet's bill, which is the project the most likely to succeed, were to pass in the Senate as it has already done in the Chamber ? In the first place, the wife would of course be emancipated from the marital power, which is not the case under the present system as we have just seen.   M. Naquet also places husband and wife on the same footing as regards adultery, which is not now the case.   But with these two exceptions, M. Naquet's bill justifies the apprehensions of its adversaries, even when the wife's interests are alone considered.   Many provisions of the code would sadly clash with her new liberty.   Divorce should be the coping of any reform of our marriage laws, not the foundation stone.

" Let us, in the first place, consider the children.   It is evident that the divorced wife does not obtain complete control over her children, especially if she remarries.   In this case she falls into the same category as the widow, whose disabilities we have already noticed.   She will still be subject to the decision of the family council as regards preserving the guardianship of her children, and will have less authority over them than the other divorced parent. Such inequality would cause her to look with disfavor upon divorce not backed by other reforms, and she would probably have less and less recourse to it.

" Furthermore, would not the possibility of divorce be a temptation to the husband to abuse the powers which the law gives him over the fortune of his wife?   At present he is required to at least provide for her wants. What limit would there be to his depredations if M. Naquet's bill passes? Many an honest lawyer will admit that the husband has a thousand ways of ruining his wife under whatever system they are married. By the dissolution of the marriage tie, the husband, after spending his wife's fortune, could disembarrass himself of her, while she would not be able to hold him to the slightest obligation.

"If now we consider the advantages of divorce, we find an aspect of the question quite peculiar to France. I refer to divorce in its relations to nullity of marriage, which modifies in this particular the narrowness of our civil code. It will be remembered that in France the civil law and canon law are absolutely distinct. The causes which make possible the nullity of a marriage are not the same in the two systems. The first, which is very severe, admits of but one case,—error concerning the person.* Our courts have decided that this means the marriage of a man or woman to another than the individual he or she had in view,—a mistake which, it may be said, never occurs. Once married, two beings are bound together for life, whatever their past has been, or whatever their future may be.

"Such was not the doctrine of the old canon law. The church of course held to the principle of the indissolubility of marriage, but of marriage normally contracted and uniting certain conditions. The theory of nullity of marriage was very liberal, there being not less than sixteen cases in which the contract could be broken. It was declared null *ab initio*, and thus the doctrine of indissolubility was left intact, while the present intoler-

* See Civil Code, Art. 180, and the commentaries on this article.

able situation, from which there is no escape, was avoided. By the re-establishment of divorce, so as to recognize exactly the causes accepted by the canon law, religious scruples would be gotten over, and those who combat the Naquet bill from church prejudices would be able to unite with its advocates. Thus, with the tolerance of Rome and the consent of the State, divorce might become a living fact again." *

I next take up the moral condition of French women. A Paris journalist has written: " It is not necessary to go to Constantinople to find the harem : one need not leave Paris, with this single difference, that instead of being confined to the narrow walls of a palace, it overflows the limits of the fortifications." † This is no exaggeration. The vital statistics published each week in the daily papers—to cite but one of many proofs—establish only too firmly the truth of this statement. I select at hazard one of these official reports. During the sixth week of 1882 there were 1,268 births at Paris, of which 937 were legitimate and 341 illegitimate.‡ That is to say, nearly one-third of all the children who come into the world each week at the French capital are born outside of wedlock,—some 17,000 bastards launched on to life annually in one city of France. In such a state of things the

---

* The general subject of the legal position of women in France, is briefly and clearly treated by M. Léon Richer in his volume entitled, the "Women's Code" (*Le code des femmes;* Paris: Dentu, 1883). I would recommend, as a convenient edition of the civil and penal codes, the two little volumes of M. Rivière (*Les codes français;* Paris: Marescq, 20 rue Soufflot). The different matrimonial systems are clearly explained in Professor Emile Acollas's interesting little book, " Marriage " (*Le mariage;* Paris: Marescq, 1881).

† M. Albert Rabou, *La France*, February 9, 1881.

‡ *Le Temps*, February 12, 1882.

France of to-day would do well to imitate the Convention, which issued the celebrated decree that "every girl who supports her illegitimate child during ten years, by the fruit of her own labor, may claim a public recompense."*

Mme. Emilie de Morsier,† than whom no woman in France is more competent to speak for the moral condition of her sex, writes me as follows: "It may be thought surprising that French women have not demanded the abolition of State regulated vice (*police des mœurs*) before advancing their claims for civil and political equality. Ought not the first protest of woman to be against a law which makes property of her very person? Her body is not her own; under certain circumstances it may become the property of the police, and an object of speculation for dealers in human flesh, whose business is protected by this same police. This law condemns women to the life of a public prostitute under the surveillance of the authorities.

"Now and then a voice has been raised against the infamies without name concealed under the hypocritical expression of the *police des mœurs*. Eugène Sue, in his 'Mysteries of Paris,' stigmatized this official sentine

---

* Legouvé, *Histoire morale de la femme*. Legouvé also cites the following ordinance of the Convention, one of the many examples of the fair treatment of women by that body: "Every mother whose work cannot support her family, may claim aid from the nation." Professor Acollas's work, "The Child Born Outside of Wedlock" (*L'enfant né hors mariage*), may be read in connection with this subject.

† Mme. de Morsier, besides taking an active part in all philanthropic and reformatory movements in France, is the translator into French of Miss Phelps's "The Gates Ajar" and "Hedged In," Mrs. Ashurst Venturi's "Joseph Mazzini, a Memoir," and of Mazzini's two essays, "The Duties of Man" and "Thoughts on Democracy."

called the 'bureau of morals' (*bureau des mœurs**), and the heart-rending life of the poor Fleur de Marie is no exaggerated invention of the novelist, but a daily actuality.   Mlle. Julie Daubié, in a little tract entitled ' The Toleration of Vice' (*La tolérance du vice*), indignantly condemns this infamous system; but this noble woman died in the midst of her campaign against immorality.

"In 1873 Mrs. Josephine E. Butler arrived in Paris. She had been for several years at the head of an English movement, whose aim was to combat this same system introduced into some parts of Great Britain by act of Parliament.   She held, with good reason, that as this curse came from the Continent, it should be denounced and attacked at its source.   Mrs. Butler was the first woman who spoke in France before large meetings on this delicate question, and those who heard her remember the profound impression she produced.

"At the same time, a Frenchman, M. Yves Guyot, spoke out against the iniquity, and began in the press a campaign, which he continued later in the deliberations of the Paris municipal council.   Having laid the responsibility for these infamies at the door of the prefect of police, he was condemned to six months' imprisonment, so that a man was the first to suffer for having championed the cause of these slaves of vice.

"Members of the British and Continental Federation for the Abolition of Prostitution, which owes its origin to Mrs. Butler, have several times visited Paris to advocate their cause, and the organization of a French committee was the result, with Mrs. Dr. John Chapman and

---

* This is the bureau of the police department, where the girls receive their cards (*cartes*), and here is the dispensary (*dispensaire*) where the doctors practice their inspection (*visite forcée*).

Yves Guyot as presidents. One might have thought that the movement, once gotten under way, would have grown in public favor. But such was not the case. Many persons were, indeed, convinced of the justice of the cause, but as soon as the novelty of the first impressions wore off, they fell back into their former state of indifference, and few passed from conviction to action. France does not yet know what self-government means. When people express the desire for a reform, they sit down, fold their arms, and wait for the government to act. It cannot, therefore, be said that there has been in this country a genuine movement of public opinion in favor of the abolition of State-regulated vice. If M. Yves Guyot had not kept up the agitation, the question would probably long ago have dropped out of sight and out of mind.

"The Paris Society for the Improvement of Public Morals (*Comité parisien pour le relèvement de la moralité publique*) follows much the same lines as the Federation, and is doing a good work.

"The various associations in France for the promotion of this cause have always been composed of men and women, but it must be admitted that it is not the feminine element which has predominated. This question, so essentially a woman's question, does not awaken their interest. It has been said that 'women make the morals,' but it would be more correct to say that they *accept* them. Through a deplorable frivolity, by a wish to please at any price, they tacitly accept men's opinions and yield to their wishes. This culpable complaisance is sometimes carried to such a length, that wives strive to imitate the dress and manners of a class in whose society their husbands occasionally find a moment's pleasure, hoping, by debasing themselves, to retain an affection which they fear may escape them. On the other hand, conscientious women, religious ones above all, scarcely dare to glance into these abysses of vice, and, brought up to believe that they have nothing to do with the outside world, say : ' These things do not concern us : men make the laws.' Selfishness, ignorance and prejudice must be great indeed, when wives and mothers do not see the depth and breadth of this question. The cause lies in the tacit acquiescence of women in the current opinions held by men on this subject of morals. They have accepted their theory of the necessity of vice, and firmly believe that the house of ill-fame is a hygienic requisite."*

There is a small body of Catholics in France, including such men as M. de Falloux, the Bishop of Amiens (M. Guilbert), and the Abbé Bougaud, who cling to the forlorn hope of conciliating Rome with the new society born of the French Revolution. But their efforts have met with no success, and every day the breach widens, the republi-

---

* The literature on this subject of public morality, especially that which treats of the grave question of State-regulated vice, has grown to immense proportions within the past few years. The *Actes du congrès de Genève* (September, 1877) and the *Compte-rendu du congrès de Gênes* (September, 1880) are rich in information on this subject. The continental organ of the Federation is *Le bulletin continental*, a monthly under the editorship of M. Aimé Humbert. These three publications may be obtained by addressing M. Humbert, 19, rue du Château, Neuchâtel, Switzerland. *La prostitution*, by Yves Guyot (Paris : Charpentier, 13, rue de Grenelle St. Germain), is perhaps the best French book on the subject. The *Westminster Review* for April, 1883, contains a paper written by Dr. John Chapman, and entitled "Prostitution at Paris," which explains very clearly and fully the system of *police des mœurs* as practiced at the French capital. M. Fallot, 17, rue des Petits-Hôtels, Paris, Secretary of the *Comité Parisien*, mentioned in the text, can furnish documents and information concerning the general condition of morals in France.

cans and freethinkers on one side, the monarchists and priesthood on the other.

This freethinking party is strong and active. On the evening of Good Friday, 1882, for example, occurred twenty-two banquets of "freethinkers and atheists" at Paris alone, and fourteen more in the environs. M. Léo Taxil's Anti-Clerical League (*Ligue anti-cléricale*) and his bold little paper entitled the *Anti-clérical*, keep up the rubadub of agitation. This rebellion against the church takes on various forms. On June 28, 1881, was founded the Civil Marriage Society (*Société du mariage civil*), with one of the mayors of Paris as its president. The great question of the separation of church and state is constantly before Parliament, and has called into existence a society and newspaper devoted specially to the advocacy of this reform. Another society is exclusively occupied with the propagandism of freethinking doctrines.

"The question of the enfranchisement of woman and the recognition of her rights," says Maria Deraismes,* "is closely connected with the anti-clerical question or freethinking movement. Woman, since the commencement of the world, has been the victim of religious tradition. It is often said that Christianity lifted woman out of her

---

* Mlle. Deraismes is one of the ablest lady speakers in France and an active leader in the anti-clerical movement. She has always been a zealous worker for women's rights, was temporary president of the Paris congress of 1878, and is to-day editor and proprietor of a strong free-thinking organ, the *Républicain de Seine-et-Oise*. Mlle. Deraismes is probably the only woman in France who is a Freemason. Her reception a year or two ago by the Lodge of Le Pecq, a small town near Paris, created no little sensation, for it was a double blow at the church, which, prohibiting even its male members from becoming Masons, could only look with holy horror on a woman's entrance into this organization. Mlle. Deraismes was president of the Paris anti-clerical congress of 1881, in which some of the most important public men of France participated.

degradation; that before the coming of Christ she was a mere thing, an object of amusement, an instrument of reproduction. But this is only a legend and has no historical foundation. The servitude of woman in antiquity has been considerably exaggerated. The fact is that she was subjected far less than many people are willing to admit.*

"The advent of Christianity scarcely modified this situation. The new doctrine condemned one sex to submit to the other; it taught that woman was made for man, and not man for woman. According to St. Paul and all the fathers of the church who came after him, women should cover their heads in the churches as a sign of submission; they are ordered to keep silence, they may not preach, they are commanded to respect their husbands, because man

---

* The divine element, according to the ideas of the ancient world, was composed of the two sexes. There were *dei feminei*, and hence temples sacred to goddesses, holy sanctuaries where were celebrated mysteries in which men were not permitted to participate. The worship of goddesses necessitated priestesses, so that women exercised the sacerdotal functions in the ancient world. The wives of the Roman consuls even offered public sacrifices to the divinities at certain festivals. This important part played by woman in the religious sphere could not but have an influence on her general position. In the Orient she put on the sovereign purple in the absence of male heirs. The modern world has not done better. Roman law permitted married women to control and enjoy their paraphernal property. The wife as well as the husband could make application for a divorce. The dramatic authors of the epoch show us that matrons exercised, when it was necessary, considerable authority in the home. The more property the wife had, the more rights she had.—M. D. "It must be admitted, although it shocks our present customs, that among the most polished peoples, wives have always had authority over their husbands. The Egyptians established it by law in honor of Isis, and the Babylonians did the same in honor of Semiramis. It has been said of the Romans that they ruled all nations but obeyed their wives. I do not mention the Sauromates, who were, in fact, the slaves of this sex, because they were too barbarous to be cited as an example."—Montesquieu, "Persian Letters," letter xxxviii.

is the head of the family as Jesus is the head of the church. Who can discover in such ordinances the elements of emancipation and equality? They are, on the contrary, a solemn and definitive proclamation of the social inferiority of woman. Christians were so uncertain as to the real value of woman, and the teachings of Jesus were so obscure on the subject, that the Council of Mâcon asked if she had a soul! Although the Virgin Mary occupies the largest place in the Catholic Church, to the exclusion of the persons of the trinity, still this preponderance of the female element in the doctrine and in the service has not improved the social condition of women.

" The French republicans of to-day are striving to establish a democracy, and they encounter on every hand a tremendous obstacle,—the church. Now of all the allies of this church, women are the most zealous, the most influential, the most numerous. They it is who have prolonged the existence of a doctrine condemned latally to disappear. Remove women from the church, and the Catholic edifice receives a mortal blow. Our men, who have so long neglected women, now begin to perceive the whole extent of the folly of which they have been guilty in refusing them knowledge. They are now trying to repair this fault. They are rapidly organizing a system of instruction for girls which shall be secular, and the same for both sexes. They see that knowledge is the source of all liberty.*

* The growing belief among French republicans that the realization or failure of their efforts to found a lasting republic in this country depends in no small measure on the women of France, is one of the most interesting features of the present political crisis. It has often been said, notably by Michelet, that women gave the death-blow to the first republic and powerfully aided the victory of the church and old beliefs. The radical publicist, M. Léon Giraud, one of the most active and intelligent friends of the women's

"Every woman who desires to obtain her rights, or who wishes at least to escape from tutelage, should second the freethinking movement. In breaking with the Catholic legend woman revokes the primordial decree which smote her, and which has rendered her an object of universal reprobation. Hence it is that freethinking makes numerous recruits among the sex which seemed doomed to be forever the prey of superstition. A large number of women are members of the anti-clerical societies, which are multiplying every day and spreading into the provinces. Turning their back on churches, they attend our gatherings, take part in the discussions and become officers of our meetings and societies. Among the many friends of this cause are women distinguished for their learning, literary talent and eloquence. I have room to name but a few, such as Mesdames Clémence Royer, Gagneur, André Léo, Angelique Arnaud, Jules de La Madélène, Edgar Quinet, Edmond Adam, Griess-Traut, Louise David, Rouzade, Feresse-Deraismes, and de Barrau."

Women participate very largely in charitable and philanthropic work. "I am happy as a French woman,"

movement in France, writes me on this subject as follows: "It is a statement which I think true and which I have tried to explain in my book 'The Romance of the Christian Woman' (*Le roman de la femme chrétienne*)." In a speech against the decrees which drove the unauthorized religious orders from France, Laboulaye said in the senate, on November 16, 1880: "If you were present at the expulsion of the congregations, you saw women praying, supplicating. Do you think they will have any affection for the republic? Hatred of the republic is becoming a feminine hatred, and a government cannot resist that." Referring to this speech a few days before his death, Laboulaye said to me in a laughing mood: "Somebody has remarked that a government is lost which has the cooks against it, because they each have a cousin in the army!"

Mme. Isabelle Bogelot* writes me, "to be able to say that our beautiful France contains many large-hearted women, and private charity is extensive. There is still much misery, for it is impossible to remove it entirely. To obtain the results we desire, and guard women from dishonor and starvation, is a problem whose solution must be sought elsewhere than in charity. I shall cite a few of these private charitable organizations at Paris, which will give an idea of the work throughout France.

"The Philanthropic Society (*Société philanthropique*), which was founded in 1780, has been a blessing to poor women for a hundred years. Among its many benefactors may be mentioned Mme. Camille Favre, whose recent liberality has made it possible for the Society to establish dispensaries for children, which will soon be opened in all the outlying quarters of Paris.† The Society for the Amelioration of the Condition of Women, already mentioned several times in this chapter, has charitable aims. The Society for Released Female Prisoners of St. Lazare (*Œuvre des libérées de St. Lazare*), founded by Mlle. Michel de Grandpré, comes to the assistance of those liberated from this well-known women's prison. Mme. de Witt has created a folding-room in connection with the extensive publishing house of Hachette & Company, which gives employment to two hundred poor women. They are fed, and the money which they deposit draws ten per cent. interest. Mme. Dalencourt has organized a society which provides needy women with

---

* Mme. Bogelot (4, rue Perrault, Paris), who is one of the most liberal-minded and active friends of the poor and unfortunate, is a member of the board of managers of the Society for Released Female Prisoners of St. Lazare (*Œuvre des libérées de St. Lazare*), of which Mme. de Barrau is director.

† The office of this society is 17, rue d'Orléans, Paris.

work and food at a very reduced price, and assures them ten per cent. on their savings. Such are a few—perhaps the most characteristic—of the Paris charitable institutions due to women and for women."

Among other benevolent works in which women participate, may be mentioned the Paris Society for the Protection of Animals, which counts many ladies among its officers and members. Female charity is sometimes of a patriotic nature, as in the case of the Association of French Ladies, which was founded in April, 1879, and whose principal object is to care for the wounded in time of war. The Association has several branch societies in the provinces and supports schools for the training of nurses at Paris and in other cities of France.

The sister of charity must not be overlooked, for in France as elsewhere she is an important factor in benevolent work. It may be said that we have in her the germ of the female physician, for in the dispensary she is a pharmacist, and at the sick-bed a doctor. The sister of charity is, therefore, acting a grand part in accustoming the public to this progressive step in the medical profession.*

---

* Concerning printed information on French charities, Mme. Bogelot writes : " *Le manuel des œuvres* (Paris : Poussielque, 15, rue Cassette), published every two years, gives an account of all public institutions and those of a private nature which have been officially recognized. *Manuel des bureaux de bienfaisance*, by Molineau (Paris : Marchal et Billard, 27, place Dauphine), is valuable. *Les gens de bien*, by Mme. Demoulin, of St. Quentin, will soon be published and, will give the names of all those who devote their attention to charity in France." M. Maxime du Camp, of the French Academy, has well described the public and private charities of Paris. For the first, see the *Revue des deux mondes*, June 15th, August 1st, September 1st and 15th, 1870, and October 15th and November 1st, 1872 ; for the second, see the same periodical, April 1st and May 15th, 1883.

In order to fully appreciate what has been accomplished in the matter of girls' instruction, we must know what was its condition when the work began. The situation previous to the Revolution may be judged by this extract from one of Mme. de Maintenon's essays on education: " Bring up your girls of the middle classes as such," she says; " do not trouble yourself about the cultivation of their minds; they should be taught domestic duties, obedience to husband, and care of children. Reading does young girls more harm than good ; books make wits and excite insatiable curiosity." As regards history, Mme. de Maintenon allows that girls should have a slight knowledge of it, in order to know the names of their own princes, so as not to mistake a king of Spain or England for a ruler of Persia or Siam. But ancient history is proscribed. " I should fear," she says, " lest those grand traits of heroism and generosity exalt their mind and make them vain and affected."

But the Revolution modified French ideas concerning women's education. A descendant of La Fontaine, Mme. Mouret, who edited a women's educational journal in 1790, read at the bar of the National Assembly a plan for the instruction of girls, which was received in most complimentary terms by the president.* It was the Convention which first spoke out clearly in France for girls' instruction. But the Convention was too short-lived to accomplish its work, and war and bad government adjourned for many long years the realization of its liberal plans.†

---

* *Dictionnaire de la presse*, p. 161.

† M. Auguste Desmoulins, the radical member of the Paris Municipal Council, in a speech at Foix, on the occasion of the unveiling of a statue to Lakanal, September 24, 1882, pointed out how this great Minister of Public

The Empire did nothing for the instruction of women, and the Restoration was worse than the Empire, for it was clerical. But the culpability of Napoleon and the Bourbons is of a negative nature. It is not the same with Louis Philippe, however. When the July monarchy, in 1833, at the instance of Guizot, created primary instruction for boys, the girls of France were entirely neglected. This was positive culpability. It must have been at this period that Balzac exclaimed: "The education of girls is such a grave problem—for the future of a nation is in the mothers—that for a long time past the University of France has not thought about it!" Efforts have since been made to remedy this fault, but there are still 3,281 *communes* which have no primary schools for girls, and 31.34 per cent. fewer girls' than boys' schools in all France.

The history of girls' intermediate instruction is still less creditable to the country. Although private initiative has nobly endeavored to supply a crying want, the State began to act but yesterday. M. Duruy, Minister of Public Instruction under the second Empire, created, in 1867, courses of lectures for the intermediate instruction of girls, but it was not until December 21, 1880, after a long and bitter struggle of three years' duration, that M. Camille Sée saw his bill become law, and France offered its girls something more than an elementary training.

Instruction under the Convention, who considered "the education of girls as indispensable as that of boys," saw his hopes, blasted in France, realized in the United States. "It is not sufficiently known," said M. Desmoulins, "that the vast system of national instruction so brilliantly consummated at this hour across the Atlantic, is the direct and natural result of all that was thought out by our encyclopedists, longed for by our grand revolution, and prepared by the National Convention."—*Bulletin de la ville de Paris*, September 30, 1882.

"Our law is at one and the same time a moral law, a social law, and a political law," said M. Sée, in the Chamber; "it concerns the future and the safety of France, for on woman depends the grandeur as well as the decadence of nations."

The manner in which this reform has been received by French women shows that they were only waiting for an opportunity to improve their minds. I cannot resist citing a few examples of their enthusiasm in what has become, in so far as France is concerned, a second Revival of Learning. The day before the Rouen College (*lycée**) opened, in October, 1882, the names of 202 girls were already on the register. The Amiens College had, during its first term, 60 day and 40 boarding scholars. At Lyons, a very clerical city, although the college opened very late in the autumn of 1882, some 40 scholars were in attendance. When the Montpellier College—the first girls' college in France—was organized, it had 76 scholars, at the end of the year more than 100, and during the autumn of 1882 the lectures were attended by 215 girls. The college at Grenoble began on April 17, 1882, with 47 girls, and in January, 1883, this number had risen to 112. This same tendency is seen in the lecture courses founded by M. Duruy, to which reference has already been made. Whereas, in 1875, these Sorbonne studies were pursued by 165 girls, in the collegiate year 1881–2 there were 244.

But the Government and the municipalities enter as heartily into the work as the women themselves. The Chamber voted, in 1882, ten millions of francs for the

---

* In the French system of secondary instruction the establishments are of two classes, those which have a State subvention and those supported entirely by the *commune*. The first are called *lycées*, the second *collèges*. I use our English word, college, for both classes.

creation of girls' colleges. Rouen, one of the first cities to demand a college, found that it would cost a million francs; the municipality forthwith contributed half that sum and the Government the other half. At the end of the first year after the promulgation of the Sée law, the following results had been obtained : The foundation of a superior normal school for women at Sèvres,* the opening of four colleges, all the preliminary steps taken to the same end in twenty-six other cities, while similar negotiations had been begun by thirty-eight other municipalities. To-day (October, 1883)—less than three years after the Sée bill became law—still greater progress can be reported, and almost every month a new girls' college is added to the vast system of public instruction in France.

University education for women was secured long before intermediate education, due mainly to the fact that no new schools had to be created. From 1866 to 1882, 109 degrees were conferred upon women in France. There have been 49 bachelors of arts, 32 bachelors of science, and 21 doctors of medicine; 98 degrees have been conferred in Paris alone. Many foreigners, especially in medicine, are found among these 109 graduates, but within the last year or two—particularly since the Sée law has created a demand for educated teachers—the number of French women studying for university degrees has greatly increased.

---

* This is a national institution corresponding to the celebrated superior normal school for men in the Rue d'Ulm at Paris. Its aim is to fit women to become directors and professors of girls' colleges. It was created July 28, 1881, at the instigation of M. Sée, by a vote of Parliament, and opened December 12 following, with about 40 scholars, ranging from 18 to 24 years. In October, 1882, 40 new scholars entered. The course of studies now covers two years, but efforts are being made to extend it to three years. The director of the school is Mme. Favre, widow of the celebrated Jules Favre.

The history of women's medical instruction in France is very significant, and shows most strikingly the growth of public opinion in regard to the higher education of women generally. In 1864 Legouvé wrote: " The reader must not think that I desire to see women mingling with male students on the seats of the law or medical school; this would indeed be a poor way to provide for their im_provement." In 1875, Dr. G. Richelot, President of the Paris Medical Society, styled the study of medicine by women "that deplorable tendency," " a malady of our epoch." But Legouvé has lived to see women sitting on the same benches with male students without detracting from the improvement of either sex, and Dr. Richelot's malady has become an epidemic. There was a time when the female students at the Paris Medical School were almost without exception from abroad. But this is not the case to-day. The first Frenchwoman to take a medical degree in France was Mlle. Verneuil, who is still practicing at Paris. She graduated from the Paris Medical School in 1870. Up to 1881 six more Frenchwomen had followed her example, five taking their degree at the capital, and one at Montpellier. Since that time several new names have been added to the list, the last being Mlle. Victorine Benoît, who was graduated at Paris in August, 1883, with the highest approval of the board of examiners, composed of such doctors as Potain, Strauss, Rendu, and Monod.

That the Paris Medical School has not shut its doors against women, in marked contrast with the action of so many other medical schools, is due in no small measure to Laboulaye. He once told me that some years ago the question of refusing women admission to the Paris Medical School was brought up in the Department of Public

Instruction. The matter was referred to him. His report to the Minister was to this effect: The rules of the school say nothing on the subject ; it would therefore seem the best and the simplest course to require of women who desire to pursue medicine the same preparatory studies and the same tests for graduation which are demanded of the male students, and thus allow both sexes to enjoy the advantages offered by the school. This sensible and just advice was followed, and the question has never been mooted since.

The co-education of the sexes is not unknown in France, although the average Frenchman, who has a very strong repugnance to the system, would be astonished at its prevalence. There are 17,728 primary schools for both sexes (*écoles-mixtes*), nearly one-third of the primary schools of France, with 633,697 scholars. They are found in every department, and there are seven in the department of the Seine. For the past thirty-two years there has been an agricultural orphan asylum for the two sexes (*asile agricole mixte*) at Cernay, in the Haut-Rhin. "These schools," says Mme. Griess-Traut, "have produced here, as in other countries, excellent results."* In the universities, co-education is accepted with scarcely an objection, and every year it becomes more and more a matter of course among professors and students alike. In fact, this rapid and hearty admission of women to the

---

* I take the figures in this paragraph from an admirable article by Mme. Griess-Traut, in the *Phare de la Loire* for November 21, 1882. The objections raised to this primary co-education, even by the most distinguished educationists of France, are always amusing and often absolutely puerile. M. Francisque Sarcey even goes to the United States to find arguments against it. In the *Dix-neuvième Siècle* for October 19, 1880, he says : "The Yankees commence to lose faith in this system, which will soon disappear " (!).

French faculties is one of the most significant and re-markable social revolutions of recent years.*

"A comparison of the condition of French literary women of to-day," says Mme. Henry Gréville,† "with

---

* Primary and intermediate co-education have become an integrant part of our American school system, but university co-education is still strongly opposed by a large class. In France, on the contrary, the first are condemned, while the second is now generally accepted. Lumping together the opinions on this subject held in the two countries, we find the system approved in the three degrees of instruction, which shows that the objections on both sides of the Atlantic are only prejudices.

A concise, learned, and very interesting account of women's education in France, past and present, and more especially of intermediate instruction, is found in *L'enseignement secondaire des filles* (Paris: Delalain, 1, rue de la Sorbonne, 1883), by M. Gréard, one of the leading educationists of France. This is the latest and most authoritative essay on the subject. Jules Simon's *L'école* (Paris: Hachette, 79, Boulevard St. Germain), while ably treating the whole subject of public instruction, devotes a large portion of his volume to a rather liberal consideration of women's education. *Histoire de l'éducation des femmes en France* (Paris: Didier, 1883), by Paul Rousselot, was awarded the Botta prize in 1883 by the French Academy. *L'enseignement secondaire des jeunes filles* (Paris: Leopold Cerf, 13, rue de Médicis), a monthly, edited by M. Camille Sée, with the co-operation of Henri Martin, Legouvé, and others, gives, besides short essays on the subject of women's education, all the current news on the question.

† Mme. Gréville (whose maiden name was Alice Marie Fleury) is the daughter of M. Jean Fleury, who was born at Vasteville, in Normandy, and is now professor at the University of St. Petersburg. She was born at Paris, Rue de Grenelle St. Germain, October 12, 1842, and is the wife of M. E. Durand, who was born at Montpellier in 1838. It will be seen, therefore, that Mme. Gréville is thoroughly French by birth as well as marriage. I give these details because she has been claimed by other countries, by Switzerland and Belgium to my personal knowledge. In 1857 Mme. Gréville went to Russia and did not return to her native land until after the Franco-German war in 1872. A few years later her literary career began in the form of remarkable novels depicting Russian society, and the *Revue des deux mondes*, the *Journal des débats*, and the *Temps* delighted their readers at one

that which they occupied during the first half of this century, presents at the very first glance a remarkable difference. What then seemed abnormal, odd, almost reprehensible, is now universally accepted without exciting any comment. In fact, from 1800 to 1850, women who had a taste for writing sought to excuse themselves before the public for indulging in this extraordinary caprice, and some, like Mme. Tastu, Mme. Ancelot, Elisa Mercœur, and Mme. Desbordes-Valmore, succeeded in being pardoned their mania by dint of good grace, amiability, I may almost say, humility. Others resembled George Sand, who came to an open quarrel with all prejudices, and lived for her art alone. Through the force of genius, she succeeded in compelling even the most recalcitrant to accept her, but only after a long and perilous struggle. Conscious of greatness and indifferent to public opinion, she was able to alleviate her vexations, but not to remove them.

"To-day a woman may write on any subject,—on science, art, and pedagogics ; she may take up fiction,—every path is open to her. The public judges her as it would a man, retaining, however, that fine, almost involuntary deference, the result of habit and good breeding, which every Frenchman—whether he shows it or not by his outward acts—feels for the woman who respects herself. This notable change, which, relatively speaking, has come about rapidly, is due principally to the fact that female writers of the present time do not entertain the same

---

and the same time with charming creations from this rapid and prolific pen. But Mme. Gréville is not only a talented and clever novelist, she is also a broad-minded, liberal thinker on all the great reform and progressive questions of the hour, and her artistic little house on the heights of Montmartre is an influential centre for the propagation of modern ideas.

ideas on literature as formerly. When a woman fifty years ago boldly took up the pen, she declared herself by this very act at variance with prejudice. Her avowed object was glory ; she desired that her name should make a noise in the world. This name, therefore, was rarely a pseudonym unless circumstances rendered a disguise necessary. From 1850 to 1880 a change, which has become the rule, took place. In order to enjoy greater liberty, almost all women who felt themselves pushed toward literature sheltered themselves behind a pseudonym, often a masculine one, whose secret was sometimes kept for many years. Their glory thus became less personal, was associated more with the talent than the individuality of the writer, was freer from alloy, and womanly dignity gained thereby. There is evidently an advantage in being discussed under a borrowed, rather than under one's real name. The family is not touched in the combats of the press, and may, up to a certain point, remain ignorant of the quarrels of literature, while, at the same time, the domestic hearth is benefited by the material rewards of literary labor. No wonder, then, that many young girls turn toward this new field of work.

" At the same moment that the prejudice against female authors began to diminish in force, a more substantial education—still far from what it should be, however—provided these literary neophytes more ample means for the attainment of their aspirations, which first assumed the form of verse, so true is it that the impulse to sing, less definite, more subtle, precedes that of speaking. Many volumes of poetry with the names of women on the title-page were born, ran their short course, and died. Then the movement became more strongly marked, took on a more precise form, and, after some groping, the feminine novel, properly so-called, was produced.* Thereby were women not only presented in a new light, but were afforded new means of existence. At the same time, numerous collections for young people were published, and a large number of distinguished women made their first literary efforts in this department. Many continue to devote themselves to juvenile literature, while others have gained a reputation in the higher walks of fiction.

"Public opinion changed so rapidly that the expressions, 'feminine studies,' 'feminine style,' were soon considered to carry with them praise rather than blame, and men even began to choose feminine pseudonyms at a time when women were borrowing their *noms de plume* from the masculine part of the calendar. But so complete a revolution was not produced without profound causes. Female authors—to cite the most important of these influences—were formerly considered, justly or unjustly, to neglect their homes so as to devote themselves more entirely to literature. The stockings in holes, the house in disorder, the children uncared for, the husband treated as an unwelcome intruder sapping the inspiration of his spouse, —all these repugnant details of domestic imperfection had passed into a proverb and brought literary women, often unmeritedly, into discredit. When the profession became the appanage not alone of a few eccentrics, but of a large recognized class of industrious, poorly paid women, it was perceived that they were, generally speaking, none the less good mothers and excellent housekeepers anxious for the reputation of the home. Their aim in taking up the pen was commonly to add some dainties to the dry bread of the daily existence of an aged mother or sick

* George Sand being an exceptional genius should be considered a precursor, not the creator of modern feminine French fiction.—H. G.

child, to come to the aid of sons who must be educated, and daughters who must be endowed. How many cases might be cited of women who, abandoned by a prodigal, unquestionably culpable husband, and reduced to the alternative of choosing between poverty and something worse, found their salvation in a return to the studies of their youth. Exhausted strength, the lack of a teacher's diploma, false pride which cannot brook an employment after having enjoyed independence, the incapacity to suffer humiliations never before experienced,—all these circumstances, singly or united, have often forced from the soul of a cruelly tried woman, cries of anguish and passion which have found an echo in the public heart. ' Where have they discovered that ?' is asked. In the tortures of a blighted existence. Hence it is that women have been able to say things which men would never have thought of or divined. The public has done them justice, believing that they do not the less merit its respect for having discreetly expressed these sufferings. This indulgence has brought into prominence a galaxy of feminine names and surrounded them with consideration and sympathy. But talent may be germinated otherwise than by misfortune. Happy souls speak in equally touching accents. The joys of the family, the frenzy of passion, and the drama of existence are subjects of study and reflection as inexhaustible for happy as for sad hearts.

"Thérèse Bentzon, Albane, the delicate author of ' Madeleine's Sin' (*Péché de Madeleine*); Juliette Lamber (Mme. Edmond Adam), Etienne Marcel, André Gérard, Georges de Peyrebrune, Jeanne Mairet,* Jacques Vincent,

---

* It is a high compliment to Jeanne Mairet that she should be classed by Henry Gréville among French authors, a compliment which may be shared by American women, for the wife of the well-known Paris journalist, Charles

and many others whose names I omit with regret, have produced works full of true sentiment and actual experience, which enable us to study the soul of the women of to-day as we never could those of the past. Other female pens have taken up philosophy and morals. The delicately penetrating reflections of Mme. Julia Daudet, her poems full of natural sentiment; the gloomy, merciful morality of Mme. Blanchecotte, who takes from humanity its afflictions, which she shares, and, whether in prose or verse, gives comfort in return; the philosophy (which rejects an invisible, unknown enemy) of Mme. Ackermann, who, standing almost alone in this order of ideas, has spoken out concerning the nature of our existence in such clear, energetic language,—such are a few of the female philosophers and moralists of the France of to-day. In another department, I may cite those clever women, *femmes d'esprit*, Daniel Darc, Ange Bénigne, and Gyp, worthy successors of Mme. de Girardin.

"The problems of education, many of which are still unsolved, could not fail to attract the attention of women, in whom the maternal sentiment is oftenest the most predominant. Mme. Pape-Carpantier's ideas on this subject gave evidence of womanly patience and good sense, and she showed the devotion of an apostle in putting them into practice. In creating object-teaching in the infant schools (*salles d'asile*) she opened her arms, like St. Vincent de Paul, to all the little ones, the hope of the future and the care of the present. But these arms were not only her own, they were those of all France. What the infant asylum (*crèche*) had done for the first months of

---

Bigot, is the daughter of Healy, the American artist. Her new novel, "Marca," was highly praised by the *Temps*, and won a prize from the French Academy in 1883.

the baby, Mme. Pape-Carpantier did for the age when the turbulent child is a danger to himself in the house, at a time when he is capable of learning a great deal in the infant-school. Object-teaching produced a large number of educational works, and gave a start to juvenile literature, which was quite backward in France, although very able women had not disdained to consecrate their time and labor to this important branch of letters. Nothing is more difficult than to address one's self to the young in language which instructs and improves, at the same time that it amuses. Mme. de Witt, *née* Guizot, followed by Mlle. L. Fleuriot, Mme. Colomb, and many others, gave themselves up to this work, often so ungrateful, and yet all the more meritorious, as it is harder, less remunerative, and does not command so much applause as the higher kinds of fiction. Pedagogics, properly so-called, have found an able expounder in the person of Mme. Coignet. And in proportion as intermediate instruction for girls is developed in our country, writers now little known will come forward to elucidate questions as yet but poorly understood. The number of young women who take degrees in science and letters increases every year, and scientific literature will undoubtedly in the near future find among them adepts of a scientific and philosophic turn of mind, such as Mme. Clémence Royer, whose works embrace a vast portion of the human thought of the present time.

" During a certain period, toward the middle of the century, a mystical tendency gave birth to writings of a lofty inspiration, which by their form almost attained to poetry. Mme. de Gasparin and Mlle. Eugénie de Guérin were the high priests of this school. But the current has changed, and these two meritorious women have left no

disciples.   Quite different is the elegant superficial literature of the society journals, in which the toilets and
pleasures of the fashionable world are described.   Mme.
de Peyronny,whose brilliant pseudonym is Etincelle,under-
stands wonderfully well the volatile art of giving form to
that which is as delicate as the wings of the butterfly. To
treat lightly light things is not an easy task, and nothing
is more difficult than to be always clever. A knowledge
of foreign languages plays an important part in our
literature, especially since the war of 1870-'71, and every
book of value published abroad has been translated into
French, generally by women. Although this kind of work
does not admit of great latitude for the development of
any individuality, Mme. Arvède Barine, by a thorough
study of Russian, German and English literatures, has
made a deserved reputation as a specialist in this department of literary labor.

" Women have not played a prominent part in French
theatrical literature. I do not mean to say, however, that
they have not the ability and desire to write plays. The
material difficulties, such as the getting up of the piece,
the rehearsals, etc., would be enough to discourage them
even if the directors were not to turn their back upon
them. At a time when the newspapers throw wide their
columns to feminine pens, *impresarios* cling to the old
prejudice and shut their doors—except in a few extraordinary instances—against every piece written by a
woman. The case of a lady is cited—and she is probably
not the only one—who, in order to have her play produced, had to hire a theatre, engage actors, and take upon
herself the responsibility of the whole representation.
She was probably more persevering and had more money
for the realization of her dream than other feminine play-

writers, since her example has not been followed. As no physiological reason has been advanced to prove that women, who are capable of contriving good novels, are incapable of making good plays, we may hope that this last prejudice will soon go to join the others in the oblivion of the past.*

"In such a short and rapid sketch I can only give the principal features of the epoch, and many names worthy of mention must be passed over for lack of space. This paper would miss its aim if I were to turn bibliographer. More important than persons is the movement, which, starting from a fixed point at the beginning of the century, is pushing on toward the hidden future of its close. In looking back at the first half of this period, it is impossible not to be struck by the marked improvement, during the past thirty years, in the literary status of French women. The future has still greater ameliorations in store for us if we continue to preserve that sense of dignity which, with very rare exceptions, characterizes to-day the female authors of France. If, at some gathering of artists or *literati*, the eye is arrested by a woman attired in tasteful simplicity, if she converses with graceful ease, if she

---

* The visitor to the Théâtre Français will notice among the large and interesting collection of busts of famous French playwrights which adorn the halls and stairways of this theatrical pantheon, the marble figures of two women, not the least of the galaxy, George Sand and Mme. de Girardin, who have added many admirable dramas to the repertory of the House of Molière. Since 1680, when the Français was founded, about sixty plays by women have been acted. Mlle. Arnaud, whose *Mademoiselle du Vigean* was given at the Français for the first time on June 28, 1883, is the latest female dramatic writer at this theatre. Dramas by women have been produced at other Paris theatres. The most recent instance is the *Autour du mariage*, a comedy in five acts, played at the Gymnase in the autumn of 1883, and due to the joint authorship of the Countess de Martel (Gyp) and M. Hector Crémieux.

knows how to listen to the recitations and the music, it is very probable that this is one of those women of whom French literature is proud. It was not safe formerly to entertain such an opinion, but blue stockings have disappeared since authoresses daily ply the needle."

"Somebody," Mme. Léon Bertaux* writes me, "has said 'Thought, daughter of the soul, has no sex.' A president of Oberlin College declared in 1867: 'While admitting that the two sexes are equally capable, I do not mean to affirm thereby that there exists no normal difference between the intelligence of women and that of men.' This incontestable diversity, this variety in the essence of expression, renders feminine art the corollary of masculine art. It is precisely in taking our stand on this precious result, that we demand for the woman, who devotes herself to art, those opportunities for elementary culture afforded by the School of Fine Arts, in order that she may possess a solid foundation on which to build her artistic conceptions. If a goodly number of

* Mme. Léon Bertaux is one of the most distinguished of modern French sculptors. Besides the statues which she has exposed during a long series of years at various exhibitions, she is the author of a number of monumental works, two frontals of the Tuileries, decorative statues for several public monuments, and a large fountain composed of eight bronze figures at Amiens. Mme. Bertaux is the only Frenchwoman who, having taken three medals in sculpture, is *hors concours*, that is to say, she may be a candidate only for the medal of honor, which is conferred each year at the annual exhibition *(salon)* on one sculptor. Mme. Bertaux is the founder and presiding genius of the Society of Female Painters and Sculptors (*Union des femmes peintres et sculpteurs*), the earliest organization of the kind in France. "The object of this international association," says Mme. Bertaux, "is to offer its members annually an opportunity to exhibit their principal works, to defend their interests, and to afford young talent a chance of making itself known."

Swedish women take an honorable position in our exhibitions and treat successfully historical subjects, it is because they have the means of developing at an early hour their artistic taste, for Stockholm has a National School of Fine Arts where women may study from the living model.*

"The interesting personality of Mme. Vigée-Lebrun (1755-1842) opens the series of the French female artists of the century. Marie Anne Elisabeth Vigée, daughter and pupil of the painter of this same name, whom she overshadowed, gave evidence in early youth of a great talent for art. At seven she is said to have drawn a man's head, full of promise for the future, and at twenty she had become celebrated for portraits commanded by the State. D'Alembert, in the name of his colleagues, gave her access to all the sittings of the French Academy, and in 1783, under the absolute monarchy, she was made a member of the Academy of Painting and Sculpture, notwithstanding the opposition of some of her future associates.

"To-day, when the female painter or sculptor is no longer looked down upon by a prejudiced society, but, on the contrary, is rather courted for her artistic talent, is it not strange that the only obstacles which she encounters are those thrown in her way by the very institutions which ought to befriend her? Does not common sense revolt against the check which they place on her

---

* That Frenchwomen are only waiting for the opportunity to participate in the valuable instruction of the School of Fine Arts is evidenced on every hand. M. Emile Guiard, for example, the secretary of the institution which he mentions, wrote me in January, 1883: "Women are admitted to the School of the Louvre (*École du Louvre*), and every one of our lectures, however dry they may be, has at least five or six female listeners."

emulation? It is true that no fixed law limits women's artistic ambition, but a hidden influence, all the more mischievous because of its disguise, militates against our success and public recognition. I shall cite but one example among a thousand. Is there a male artist of the ability of our great portrait-painter, Mme. Nélie Jacquemart, who has not been awarded a first-class medal and membership in the Legion of Honor?* The directors of the Department of Fine Arts, who have succeeded each other from time to time, have been influenced by prejudice and arbitrary routine rather than by equity, so that, since the foundation of the Third Republic, they have systematically refused female artists this important honor. The wrong is increased by the advantages enjoyed by men, for whom the country has smoothed the way, permitting them, without expense, to reap the benefits of the School of Fine Arts until their thirtieth year, if necessary, while, at the same time, the female painters and sculptors pay their portion of the taxes for the support of an institution which is an obstacle to them throughout their whole career.† It is easily understood, therefore, that the female

---

*. Mme. Bertaux herself presents a striking instance of this same injustice. Sculptors of far less merit were long ago made members of the Legion of Honor. To fully appreciate the importance of this exclusion, it should be remembered that these distinctions are very highly valued in France. But fifteen women, by the way, are members of the Legion of Honor.

† The justice of Mme. Bertaux's complaint can be fully appreciated only by those who have carefully examined the question. A French male artist who is not a graduate of the State School of Fine Arts, who is not a member of the State Academy of Fine Arts, who stands outside of the authorized official circle, labors under the greatest difficulties. The annual art exhibition, which up to 1882 had been controlled by the State, passed, in that year, into the hands of an independent body of artists (*Association des artistes français*). The prime cause of this change was the desire to escape as much as possible the evil influence of an official art *coterie*. If the male artists of

artist, who is unequally armed for the combat, and whose honors are not adjudged after the same rules of merit, occupies only a secondary place in France. These difficulties explained, the talent of the individuals mentioned in these notes stands out all the more prominently.

"The number of women still living who have received official medals since 1824 is not less than fifty-five, of whom three are sculptors and four engravers. The three sculptors are Mme. de Fauvau, Mlle. Thomas, and the author of these notes. Mme. Felicie de Fauvau, who received a medal of the second class in 1827, was one of that galaxy of romantic artists who substituted for the bad classic school of the Restoration a rather character-less style, which may be called—if we may be pardoned the pleonasm—neo-renaissance. Mlle. Mathilde Thomas, an animal sculptor of great merit, received a third class medal in 1881.* Among the forty-eight painters who have taken medals, the name of Rosa Bonheur is most

France found the yoke unbearable, it is easy to imagine what the female artists suffer, who have against them not only the State but also the extra-State organization. It must not be inferred, however, from what has just been said, that female artists are entirely ignored. The following women took honors at the *Salon* of 1883 : Second class medal, Mme. Demont-Breton, who also received a gold medal at the Amsterdam Exhibition of 1883 ; third class medal, Mlle. Lucie Contour and Mlle. Léonie Valmon ; honorable mentions : Mme. Fanny Prunaire, *née* Colonny, Mlle. Blau, of Vienna ; Mme. Van Marcke-Diéterle, Mme. Hélène Luminais, Mme. Lavieille, Mme. Marie Bashkirseff, of Russia ; Mme. Signoret, Mme. Bénard, Mlle. Delattre, a pupil of Mme. Bertaux ; Mlle. Lancelot, and Mme. Desca. This list includes painters, sculptors, engravers, etc. The last five names are those of sculptors. The State purchased the work of two of these artists. In the summer of 1883, Mlle. Martin finished the bust of Le Verrier, which had been ordered by the French Academy of Sciences.

* At least one female sculptor has the honor of being represented in the collection of art at the Théâtre Français—Fanny Dubois Davesnes, the author of the bust of the once famous dramatist, Marivaux.

widely known, although the talent of a young artist, Mme. Demont-Breton, whose fine canvas, "The Beach," (*La plage*) secured a second-class medal at the *Salon* of 1883 and was purchased by the State, places her in the front rank. Mlle. Bonheur studied under her father, and her first work seemed to give promise of a sculptor. It was a fine study in plaster of a bull that thus early revealed the solid qualities of the future artist. In 1848 she produced her masterpiece, 'Nivernese Ploughing' (*Labourage Nivernais*), which is found in the Luxembourg, and in 1865 the Empress bestowed upon her the Cross of the Legion of Honor.*

"But there is ground to hope that in a very near future women will experience in the career of arts a juster treatment; opportunities for study similar to those enjoyed by men, a school of fine arts, the prize of Rome as a stimulant, and the same artistic and official distinctions. I should also demand, although this will not be so generally accepted, that women form part of the juries at our art exhibitions.† The success of the public exhibitions of the Society of Female Painters and Sculptors proves that the victory is socially won. The second exhibition, that of 1883, occurred in the Palais de l' Industrie, the same edifice in which the great annual *Salon* displays its vast international art collection. This is an important and significant concession. It means that the day is indeed approaching when Frenchwomen will be on an exact

* I must pass over in silence many female artists of talent, such as Mlle. Élodie La Villette, the marine painter ; Mlle. Berthe Wegmann, the historical and portrait painter ; and Mme. Euphémie Muraton, the painter of still life.—L. B.

† Mlle. Thérèse Schwartze was a member of the jury on Fine Arts at Amsterdam in 1883. This is the first time in the history of international exhibitions that a woman has held such a position.

equality with Frenchmen in everything pertaining to that grandest of studies, the Fine Arts."

" One of the principal careers open to women," writes Mlle. Laure Collin,* " is the honorable and modest calling of teacher, and especially teacher of music, in which department large numbers have distinguished themselves. Most of these successful teachers are graduates of the well-known Paris Conservatory, which is open, when vacancies occur, to every woman under twenty, who possesses the necessary means, and who can pass the competitive examinations.†

---

* Mlle. Laure Collin, the author of several admirable manuals on musical subjects, may be considered to be the presiding genius of musical instruction in the French public school system. She is professor in the Girls'. Superior Normal School at Fontenay-aux-Roses, the Normal School for Mistresses of the Seine at Paris, and the Normal Courses for Maternal Schools, at Sceaux and Paris, where she teaches a remarkable and very successful method approved by the Minister of Public Instruction. Mlle. Collin is also the author of a history of music.

† As several American girls have already studied with success at the Conservatory, and as others doubtless contemplate following their example, I subjoin some remarks on this institution which Mlle. Collin has been kind enough to furnish me. "The Conservatory," says Mlle. Collin, " is a school of high virtuosity. To keep one's place is almost as difficult as to get admitted to the school, for it is absolutely necessary, under penalty of expulsion, to pass the periodic examinations. This requirement forces talents to multiply and develop, I hardly know how, for there is no uniform method pursued, each professor being free to apply his own, if he has one. But I explain the success of the institution in this wise. There are families of artists, forming a sort of privileged class, in which virtuosos succeed each other generation after generation, and the children, while at their play, so to speak, imbibe good musical traditions. The girls who fill the classes of the Conservatory come generally from these families. Let us take a student of ordinary ability and follow her step by step from the moment she enters the school. If a member of one of the three or four elementary classes, she will have to undergo the trimestrial examinations, when her progress will be

" France possesses many talented female pianists. Léonie Tonel—a very exceptional case—was unanimously awarded a certificate by the Conservatory jury of admission, her remarkably skilful execution exempting her from the competitive examination. One of our most celebrated pianists was Mme. Pleyel, *née* Moke, a pupil of Jacques Herz, Moscheles and Kalkbrenner. After playing with great success in all the capitals of Europe, she became, in 1847, professor at the Brussels Conservatory, and died in Belgium in 1875. Mme. Farrenc, whose death occurred a few years ago, was also a pupil of Moscheles, Hummel and Reicha, and was distinguished as a composer, writer and virtuoso. In 1869 the Institute awarded her the Chartier prize for the best compositions of music. Mme. Farrenc's class at the Conservatory has turned out

---

ascertained and promotion into the upper classes will follow. Her aim must now be to secure prizes awarded at the public competitions which occur in the month of July. These examinations consist in the execution of a piece of music designated beforehand by the jury, and the reading at sight of an unpublished piece. The first is the same for all the competitors, but its interpretation varies according to the style of the different professors, for it is evident that the pupils of M. Delaborde will give another rendering than those of M. Lecouppey or Mme. Massart. The fate of the pupil depends upon the result of these public competitions. She may try three times, a year apart. If she secures, the third year, an honorable mention, for example, she has two more trials, but is pitilessly dropped from the Conservatory after two new successive failures. The professors, of course, look with most favor on pupils endowed with a talent for execution and capable of shining at these musical tourneys. But it often happens that the unsuccessful students succeed better as teachers than their more fortunate companions. It has been the custom during the past ten years for Mme. Erard to present the winner of the first prize one of her pianos, while the Pleyels do the same for the second prizeman. The present director of the Conservatory, M. Ambroise Thomas, has introduced many changes in the curriculum of studies, and to-day the pupils receive a most complete musical and dramatic education."

a legion of good female pianists. Among our most highly appreciated contemporaries, I may mention Mesdames Massart, Josephine Martin, Montigny-Rrémaury, whose talent for execution is very remarkable, and among the number of those who have secured a first prize at the Conservatory, and who follow the modest calling of teacher, I may name Hortense Parent, who has struck out a new path and founded a normal school for the piano, which has rendered great service to extra-State instruction.

"Among celebrated singers, who, though dead, are not forgotten, I may cite Mesdames Cinti Damoreau, Dorus-Gras, Nau, and Stolz, all of whom became famous at the opera; Mlle. Falcon, whose magnificent voice, lost, alas! so soon, has not yet had its equal; Mme. Vandenheuvel-Duprez, cut down in her prime and at the zenith of her success; Mme. Cabel, who, although Belgian by birth, won naturalization on the stage of the Opéra Comique; Mesdames Marie Sasse, Gaymard, Darcier, Wertheimber, and Delagrange; Mme. Gallimarié, who gave such an original creation to so many rôles; that eminent artist, whom we are still permitted to enjoy, and whose style is marked with such rare distinction, — Mme. Miolan-Carvalho; Mme. Bilbaut-Vancheld, whose first-rate talent immediately placed her in the front rank; and lastly, that brilliant singer, eclipsed after shining an instant like a meteor, —Mme. Adler Devriès.*

"I must not forget two celebrated female musicians of quite different styles, Mesdames Viardot and Ugalde.

* The name of Mme. Adler Devriès, a native of Holland, reminds me of several other foreigners who have made a reputation in France, as Sophie Cruvelli (the Baroness Vigier), who gave new life to Spontini's *Vestale;* Krauss, who is to-day our leading operatic singer; the Countess de Sparre and the Countess Merlin, whose sweet voices charmed drawing-rooms at the time when Malibran electrified the public at the Italian Theatre.—L. C.

Auber said of the latter, 'She would have invented music,' and Charles de Bernard pretended that she must have been born in a piano. This was indeed almost true, for Delphine Beaucé (who became at sixteen Mme. Ugalde), a pupil of her mother and her grandfather, the composer Porro, won a medal, when six years old, in a competition, where she performed a part in a composition for two pianos. She taught music at nine, and three years later sang the mezzo-soprano solos in concerts given by the Prince of Moscow. Her voice soon developed into a soprano of great compass. Her *début* in 1848 at the Opéra Comique in the *Domino noir* created a sensation. Engaged several times by this theatre and by the Lyrique, Bouffes, Porte St. Martin, Châtelet, she created twenty-one important rôles. Mme. Ugalde (married in 1866 to M. Varcollier) has for several years devoted herself to teaching, and no one has had greater success in forming artists for the lyric stage. Marie Sasse, for example, is one of her pupils.

" Mme. Viardot (Pauline Garcia), daughter of the Italian singer Manuel Garcia, goddaughter of Paër, and sister of Malibran, is, beyond question, one of the greatest artists of our epoch. Her sweet mezzo-soprano voice, supported by a masterly style, has breathed new life into the *Orphée* and *Alceste* of Gluck, which had too long lacked that powerful interpretation without which they fail. Mme. Viardot has been heard in all the great cities of Europe and has sung in the language of each country she visited. Among her most remarkable creations are Gounod's Sappho and Fidès in *Le Prophète*. She has had for some time a class at the Conservatory, and is the author of several unpublished partitions.

" Several Frenchwomen have taken up operatic composition and some of them have succeeded in it. At their head stands Louise Bertin, who, shortly after the appearance of Victor Hugo's ' Notre Dame of Paris, ' composed an opera, *Esmeralda*, the subject of which was drawn from this book. Mme. Tarbé des Sablons is the author of two operas, *Les Bataves* and *Les Brigands*, founded on Schiller. Mme. Pauline Thys has written an opera in four acts entitled *Judith,* and several operettas which were well received. Mme. Olagnier composed, a short time ago, a very original comic opera, *Le Saïs*, which had a great success, Capoul creating the principal rôle.*

" In the symphonic style of composition I must again mention Mme. Farrenc (aunt of M. Reyer of the Institute), the author of a symphony which was performed at the Conservatory and much admired. I may further name the Baroness de Maistre, the Countess de Grandval,† who has composed some fine religious and instrumental music; Augusta Holmès, who has written a symphony, *Les Argonautes;* and lastly, Mlle. Chaminade, whose very remarkable compositions were executed in 1882 at the Pasdeloup concerts in Paris.

" In ballad music I must recall the names, forgotten today, of Pauline Duchambge, a master in this department of music, and of that other well-known artist, Loïsa Puget (Mme. Gustave Lemoine) who followed her. Mlle. Puget was the author of her own ballads, which she sang with great charm and spirit. Mme. de Rothschild is the author

---

* " If an opera by a woman succeeds, I am delighted, for it is a confirmation of my little system that women are capable of doing everything we do, with this single difference between them and us, that they are more amiable than we are."—Voltaire, October 18, 1736, to Mr. Berger, director of an opera-house.

† Mme. de Grandval was awarded in 1883 the prize offered by the Minister of Fine Arts at the competition of the Society of Composers.

of a sweet melody which all Paris sang, and Pauline Thys, whom I have already mentioned, has shown talent for ballad music. The refined drawing-room of Mme. Marjolin, daughter of Ary Scheffer, was recently charmed with the melodies of an artist of great merit, Mlle. Wild, a pupil of Barbereau. Her style is large and pure. She has written several masses, among others a pastoral mass, some remarkable hymns, and pieces for the organ. She composed almost, at her *début*, a quatuor for string instruments which won the approbation of masters like Onslow.

"I have spoken of some of the leading female teachers of the piano, and I have now to mention what we have done in vocal instruction. Eugénie Chauvot, a pupil of Duprez, has secured a high place as professor of singing, and has grouped about her the most distinguished artists. Mme. Féret, a pupil of Révial, whose poor health greatly limits her work, has carefully collected the excellent principles of the master and transmitted them to her disciples. French women play also an important part in the musical instruction given in the public and normal schools. The author of these notes has labored in this field.* The popularizing of musical instruction has made great progress in the last few years, and its development bids fair to soon place France on a level with the nations the most favored in this respect. I am proud to say Frenchwomen have contributed to this progress in the most remarkable and efficacious manner."

"I may say, without exposing myself to the imputa-

---

* I have witnessed with astonishment the wonderful results of Mlle. Collin's method, and I do not hesitate to recommend its careful examination to the teachers in our American schools, where the science of music is too often sacrificed to the learning by ear of a few patriotic songs.

tion of indulging in national vanity," writes M. Paul Foucart,* "that in no other country of Europe does woman, in proportion as her situation requires it, work as much as in France; that nowhere does she, in every grade of society, associate herself so closely and effectively with the husband in his efforts to assure the moral and material prosperity of the family. Those foreigners who have learned, by a long residence in France, to understand the country, are powerfully struck by this fact. 'No housewives are more perfect than the French,' says Karl Hillebrand,† 'who, without boasting of being housekeepers after the German fashion, know how to superintend domestic affairs with a judicious and firm hand. Many of them even take the husband's place in business. . . Ambitious to the highest degree, passionate under a cloak of coldness, clever in what they undertake, elegant in appearance, endowed by nature with a grace carefully cultivated by a skilful education, possessing above all a firm character and a strong will, they direct husband as well as brother or son, urge him on, smooth his way, and take all the necessary and difficult steps to secure his success. In a word, they conquer him a place in the world and help him to defend it.' ‡

"The most natural and legitimate method of securing

---

* M. Paul Foucart, of Valenciennes, is a close student of industrial questions in France, and is the author of a pamphlet entitled the "Industrial Function of Women" (*Fonction industrielle des femmes*), the substance of which was given as a lecture at Havre in 1880.

† "France and the French during the Second Half of the Nineteenth century" (*La France et les français pendant la seconde moitié du XIXe siècle*), Chapter I.—P. F.

‡ I do not pretend that there are not exceptions to Karl Hillebrand's complimentary estimate of Frenchwomen, but these exceptions are much rarer than people generally imagine.—P. F.

that grand *desideratum* of society, the division of labor, would be for the women of all classes, supported by the men, to devote themselves entirely to household duties. But almost always among the lower classes, women are forced to seek occupations directly remunerative, which, on account of the brusque development of the great industries and the exactions of a fierce competition, compel them to confide their children to mercenary or charitable institutions, thus inflicting on the family, in exchange for insignificant pecuniary gains, incalculable moral losses.

" Without believing that the world is degenerating and that the ideal of humanity must be sought in the past, I hold that before the advent of the industrial revolution born of the general use of steam machinery, the condition of the women of the lower classes was, in certain respects, more normal than it is to-day. Manufactories employing hundreds of hands were then very rare, while many occupations—spinning, lace making, tulle work, the weaving of muslin, the reeling and weaving of silk, the sorting, picking and winding of wool bobbins, etc.,—were followed at home. In this way women gained at the domestic hearth a sum which considerably augmented the resources of the family, without depriving it of maternal care and influence. If young girls left the paternal roof, it was only to labor in the fields, to become servants, or to work as apprentices in small shops,—callings in which agility, address, or taste were the all-important requisites.

" Toward the second third of the nineteenth century were felt for the first time with all their force, the consequences of a production which developed more rapidly than the demand, and which occasioned stoppage and famine where its promoters predicted abundance. Weeks without work for the husband and misery at home ! How is the family to be kept from starvation? Many wives imagined that the shop, the cause of the evil, might also prove its remedy. If the husband and wife were both at work would not the home realize twice as much, at least in ordinary seasons? And when the hard times came, it was not probable that all industries would be affected; when the shops stopped, it would be rare if both husband and wife were thrown out of work. Will not life therefore be made easier? The answer to this question is found in the following table,* published in 1882, by the minister of commerce, which gives the actual wages of those employed in textile industries in France.

		Ordinary Wages.	Maximum Wages.	Minimum Wages.
Spinning.	Cotton,	1.78	2.29	1.40
	Wool,	1.71	2.15	1.37
	Silk,	1.61	2.04	1.34
	Hemp and Flax,	1.68	2.19	1.38
	Averages,	1.69	2.17	1.36
Weaving.	Cotton,	2.03	2.66	1.64
	Wool,	1.82	2.31	1.56
	Silk,	1.75	2.41	1.33
	Hemp and Flax,	1.69	2.19	1.36
	Averages,	1.82	2.39	1.47

" It appears, therefore, that it is for the miserable pittance of one franc and eighty-two centimes† that so many

---

* This table is taken from the " Statistical Annual of France " (*Annuaire statistique de la France*) for 1882.—P. F. The money figures in this and the tables which follow are in francs and centimes. A franc equals about nineteen cents, and a centime about a fifth of a cent.

† About thirty-five cents in American money. It may be considered, however, that thirty-five cents has the purchasing power in France of at least fifty cents in the United States.

women abandon home and children, thus doing a great injury to themselves as well as to those women who cling to the old customs. The competition of the factory has reduced the price of manual labor in many industries still practiced at home. Embroidery and hand-made lace, for example, although they have much declined, continue to give employment, the first to 150,000, and the second to about 220,000, women. The pay of an ordinary embroiderèr in the Vosges has fallen to one franc and ten centimes, while the apprentice of fourteen, who copies only simple easy models, earns one-half that amount.* Still worse is the condition of lace-makers. At Valenciennes, of which they were formerly one of the glories, they have entirely disappeared. At Alençon, in Auvergne, at Chantilly, at Bayeux, they earn only from one to one and a half francs, and it is probable that all of these poor souls will have to soon lay aside their bobbins unless they wish to die of hunger.

"In the workshops of the small manufacturers the situation is scarcely any better, as is shown by the careful investigations made by the Paris Chamber of Commerce in 1860. At that time 106,310 women were employed in the various industries of the capital. The Chamber of Commerce divided them into three classes according to their occupations and wages :

First Division.	1,176	women earning	0.50
	2,429	"	"	0.75
	6,505	"	"	1.00
	7,013	"	"	1.25
	17,203			

---

* Augustin Cochin, " Monograph on the Workingwoman of the Vosges " (*Monographie sur l'ouvrière des Vosges*).—P. F.

Second Division.	16,722	women earning	1.50
	7,644	"	"	1.75
	24,810	"	"	2.00
	7,723	"	"	2.25
	17,273	"	"	2.50
	2,955	"	"	2.75
	7,588	"	"	3.00
	411	"	"	3.25
	2,250	"	"	3.50
	1,264	"	"	4.00
	88,340			
Third Divison.	278	"	"	4.50
	270	"	"	5.00
	146	"	"	6.00
	73	"	"	7 to 10
	767			

"If we leave out of the account the first of these three divisions, composed principally of girls under sixteen and of women whose aim is simply to add to their own comfort or supplement their husband's salary by needle-work, and who are often lodged and boarded; and if, for quite different reasons, we do not take into consideration the third division, made up of women who enjoy exceptionally high wages,—the second division will alone furnish the data with which to arrive at the average pay of Parisian working-women, engaged chiefly in the important departments of tailoring and the manufacture of textile fabrics. It appears that this average is two francs and fourteen centimes a day,—a small sum; greater, however, than the reality, as M. Leroy-Beaulieu has proved by pointing out certain elements which had been neglected in the calculation.*

* "Women's Work in the Nineteenth Century" (*Le travail des femmes au XIXe siècle*), first part, Chapter IV.—P. F. Mme. Caroline de Barrau also has shown, in her able "Essay on the Wages of Women at Paris" (*Étude sur le salaire du travail féminin à Paris*) that the average pay of working-

" Since 1860, on account of the increased depreciation of money and the corresponding rise in the price of food, these figures have gone up a little. But the following table, taken from the statistical publication for 1882 already referred to, which places Paris side by side with the capitals of the departments, shows how small this increase has been :

DAILY WAGES, WITHOUT BOARD, OF A WORKING-WOMAN IN THE SMALL INDUSTRIES.

	1. AT PARIS.			2. IN THE CAPITALS OF THE DEPARTMENTS.		
	Usual.	Maximum.	Minimum.	Usual.	Maximum.	Minimum.
Washer-women ...3.00		3.50	2.50	1.70	2.09	1.47
Embroiderers 3.00		4.00	2.50	1.69	2.19	1.36
Corset-makers 2.00		3.50	1.50	1.60	2.08	1.28
Dress-makers.....2.00		4.00	1.50	1.62	2.06	1.35
Pantaloon-makers.4.00		6.00	3.00	1.62	2.08	1.30
Lace-makers......3.00		4.50	2.00	2.03	2.57	1.56
Artificial flower-makers 3.00		3.50	1.50	1.87	2.45	1.51
Vest-makers 3.00		4.00	2.00	1.65	2.08	1.32
Makers of linen garments 2.00		3.50	1.50	1.45	1.83	1.20
Milliners 2.00		3.50	1.50	1.49	2.03	1.20
Sewers on shoes..3.00		4.50	2.00	1.66	2.10	1.30
Averages 2.80		4.10	2.00	1.67	2.14	1.35

" Less than three francs at Paris and less than two francs in the chief towns of the provinces,—such are the daily wages of working-women in the small industries of France. And it must be further borne in mind that this

women is far below the figures given in the statistics. She considers it even under two francs. M. Othenin d'Haussonville (*Revue des deux mondes*, April 15, 1883, p. 859) says : " Having noted the large number of women who earn but two francs or less than two francs, I am led to believe that Mme. de Barrau is right."

pittance becomes still more beggarly, or is reduced to nothing, in moments of sickness, during a dead season or complete stoppage. To the wife whose husband also earns something, it is a very appreciable help; for the virtuous girl or widow it is scarcely enough to keep body and soul together; for the woman who has family cares —aged parents to support, young children to bring up— it is the source of terrible misery, mendicity or prostitution.

"Such is the present condition of things in France, similar to that found in many other countries in Europe. The picture of the fearful consequences of this situation has been often drawn, especially by Jules Simon * and Leroy-Beaulieu,† and I myself have endeavored to suggest the moral and material remedies for the disorder."‡

French socialism, at all epochs and under every form, has always been more or less friendly to women. The working-men's congresses of late years have passed resolutions in favor of giving women the same pay as men for the same work, and, in some instances, demanding their political equality. But the dreams of theorists and

---

* " The Working-woman " (*L'ouvrière*).—P.F. Jules Simon's book tends to this conclusion : Woman should be the guardian of the domestic hearth, and man alone should go forth into the world to win the daily bread.

† " Women's Work in the Nineteenth Century " (*Le travail des femmes au XIXe siècle*).—P. F.

‡ " Women's Industrial Function " (*Fonction industrielle des femmes*).—P. F. The State employs women in but one department, if I am not mistaken. A chief clerk of the Minister of Posts and Telegraphs informs me that 5,500 females are engaged in France in the postal and telegraphic service. They are paid from 800 to 1,800 and 2,000 francs a year, and at the end of a certain period are retired on a pension. The sale of tobacco, which is a government monopoly, is entirely in the hands of women. No man is ever given a tobacco shop in France.

the resolutions of public assemblies have found their realization, probably, in but one instance,—the remarkable Social Palace at Guise.

M. Godin* writes me : " The foundation of the *Familistère* reposes on principles which are a synthesis of the practical ideas forced upon the attention of the world by the St. Simonian, phalansterian and communistic schools of the early part of this century. But it is above all for women and children that our creation at Guise has proved a happy event. The Association of the *Familistère* is, I think, the only institution which has, up to the present time, put into practice respect for the rights of women, who are treated as the equal of men in all the affairs of life. This idea of the equality of the sexes was borrowed from Fourier. The *Familistère* could not change the laws of French society, but, as members of the Association, women enjoy all the rights of men. They may aspire to all the honors at the disposal of the Asso-

---

* In order not to endanger the success of the *Familistère*, M. Godin felt constrained for many years to hold aloof from public affairs. But in 1870 he broke a long silence by publishing a manifesto, in which he vigorously attacked the Imperial *plébiscite* of that year and predicted the misfortunes it was to entail on France. A month later M. Godin was chosen a member of the Council General (*conseil général*) of the Department of the Aisne. When the Franco-German war burst upon the country, he, as mayor of Guise, firmly protected the interests of the city against the exorbitant demands of the enemy. Elected in February, 1871, a member of the National Assembly, M. Godin sat five years on the liberal republican (*Union républicaine*) side of the Chamber. He retired from national politics in 1876, but has always retained his seat in the Council General of the Aisne. In the midst of political and industrial occupations, M. Godin has found time for literary work. The ideas so briefly treated in the text are fully developed in a number of valuable volumes on social questions, but more especially in "Government, What it has Been, What it Ought to Be, and True Socialism in Action " (*Le gouvernement, ce qu'il a été, ce qu'il doit être, et le vrai socialisme en action*).

ciation; they are electors and eligible; they may form a part of all committees and councils. They perform these duties with faithfulness, and have shown themselves inaccessible to cabal, which has not always been the case with the men.

"In order that women may profit by the social liberty to which the present current of ideas is leading them, a change must be made in the system of family life: domestic economy must be modified and perfected. The emancipation of women will remain in the domain of speculation, as long as our institutions and customs impose on the father and mother the entire responsibility of the care of the family. The *Familistère* has solved this problem by assuming the bringing up of the children from the moment of their birth, so that the mother has to bestow on them only her milk and caresses, and the family, its tenderness and affection. But even in the absence of mother and family the children are not neglected. They always receive the closest attention. At every stage of their growth the children are under the eye of the Association. Separated into nine divisions in nine different rooms, each division has its nurses and teachers, who give instruction in keeping with the age of their pupils. In this way the mother and father can confer on their offspring the delights of family life, without inflicting on them, at the same time, any of its discomforts. The care and education of the children—which are the same for both sexes—being thus assumed by the Association, the duties of maternity are reduced to nursing during the early months of the child, and the mother is not hindered from attending to her other occupations. Women, therefore, find themselves emancipated, in so far as they desire it, from one of the most monopolizing obligations; they recover their liberty and may devote themselves to work and culture.

"In order to introduce this innovation, it is indispensable that the isolated habitation give place to the common dwelling, the phalanstery or social palace, so that the bringing up of children may be made a distinct organized part of the family system. The *commune*, therefore, must be architecturally reformed, and all the common household duties be placed in proximity to the home. It is necessary, furthermore, to bring about the division of domestic labor; to establish for the children a nursery, infant schools, primary schools, etc.; to organize kitchens, laundries, public halls, etc. Only in this way is it possible to reconcile household duties and family cares with the exercise, on the part of women, of civil and political rights and lucrative employments."

CHAPTER II

BELGIUM.

BY ISALA VAN DIEST, M.D.

[Miss Isala Van Diest began her medical studies at Bern, Switzerland, in April, 1874. In order to prepare herself for the new work, she had already spent some time in Germany, mastering the language, mathematics and Latin. "I had a strong taste for the sciences," Miss Van Diest writes me, "and especially for chemistry, which opens such a vast field for theorizing, and I determined to take the degree of doctor of sciences." This she did in 1876 at Bern, and next turned her whole attention to medicine, securing the degree of M.D., in May, 1879, from the same university. Her thesis for the doctorate of sciences was an "Essay on the Gonolobus Condurango" (*Etude sur le gonolobus condurango*), a substance much praised in America for its curative effects on the cancer; that for the doctorate of medicine was entitled, "Hygiene in Prisons" (*Hygiène des prisons*). "I chose this subject simply as a pretext," Miss Van Diest says, "in order that I might expose my views concerning man's responsibility for crime, and that I might have an opportunity of criticising the repressive system in vogue in the Swiss penitentiaries." Besides these two theses, Miss Van Diest has published anonymously some essays on social questions. "Conscious of the great moral influence which the physician who relieves physical suffering exercises over women," Miss Van Diest remarks, "I decided to study medicine as a means of opening their hearts to me, and of exhorting them to throw off their apathy, to help each other, and to demand the rights which belong to them. My efforts are very limited, the struggle has only begun, and I shall probably not live to see the end. But if it be permitted me only to see the question taken up in every country, and above all in my native land, where such powerful causes are at work to hold women in subjection, I shall die happy, certain of the triumph of our cause in a not too distant future." Miss Van Diest is the first and only female physician in Belgium. But she cannot secure the authorization which will allow her to practice. "I fear that I shall soon be obliged to give up the fight," she wrote me recently, "and go to France, England or Holland, unless I wish to lose the fruit of all my studies."]

THE situation of woman in Belgium is about the same as in France. The manners and customs of the two countries resemble each other, and the same code, which regulates the conduct and rights of civil life, governs both nations. In Belgium, even more so than in France, the condition of the women of the lower classes is very unfortunate. In our great industrial centres, woman at the tenderest age becomes the slave of the most brutalizing labor. Who has not witnessed with sorrow in our manufacturing cities the stream of workers—poorly dressed women and children, with their pale, wan, thin faces—moving slowly on and disappearing behind the gates of our factories? Shut up in these prisons from early morning until night, with scarcely an hour's repose during a long day, they breathe a foul, mephitic atmosphere, surcharged with miasma, steam and dust. Placed in the midst of the deafening noise of the machinery, the whirlwind of belts, flies and wheels, the slightest imprudence or thoughtlessness, a misstep, may cost the loss of a limb if not of life itself. Our large cities contain many such cripples of labor.

Family life does not exist for these miserable creatures. Constantly separated from her children, how can the mother give them the necessary care? Poverty and fatigue plunge her into such a state of moral and physical helplessness, that she can do nothing to improve the lot of her offspring. As soon as the child is old enough, he follows his mother to the factory. These poor children receive no instruction. Their mental, like their physical development, is entirely sacrificed because of the miserable pay which their week's toil produces. Death reaps a rich harvest here, and those who chance to escape its ravages are etiolated from their earliest youth.

From a moral point of view, the workshop is a loathsome centre for women. Ignorant, with no idea of the difference between right and wrong, without a check or guide, how can these poor souls resist vice? Is it necessary to describe all the terrible consequences and endless sufferings and misery which such a condition entails on girls of the lower classes?

Many well-known voices have been repeatedly raised in Belgium to protest against this state of things. Several other countries long ago regulated by legislation the employment of women and children in factories. In Germany the minimum age for the constant employment of children is ten years, while in France it is twelve years. No such law exists in Belgium. Nearly ten years ago, at the instigation of the Royal Academy of Medicine, a bill was laid before our Chamber of Deputies concerning the employment of women and children in factories. But up to the present time (1883) it has never been acted upon. The National Hygienic Congress, held at Brussels in 1852, the press and a large number of savants and publicists have demanded, and are still demanding, a reform in this direction. But all in vain. As far back as 1843 the government ordered an inquiry concerning the labor of women and children in the mines. Competent authorities were consulted,—chambers of commerce, engineers and medical commissions, and all recommended their exclusion from this terrible field of work. The report revealed all the sad evils of the situation. It established beyond question what everybody had already said and repeated a thousand times, viz., that women are not made for the hard labor of miners, that their employment in the mines is the cause of unspeakable depravity and disorder, and that it has as a result the degeneration of the population. The report of the medical commission of the Province of the Hainaut declares, that those who employ women and girls in mines are guilty of an abuse which disgraces humanity and which no pretext can justify. Years have passed since then, but the demands and protests of our own countrymen and women, as well as the examples set by foreigners, have accomplished nothing,—a striking instance of the difficulty which a question of humanity and justice encounters in the effort to prevail over an evil.

The poor girl of the country is also sacrificed. There, too, her toil is a source of speculation and her interests are quite forgotten. Many townships of Flanders have their convents which, while pretending to be schools for instruction in reading, writing and the catechism, are in reality only workshops where little girls are taught to make lace. Children as young as five or six years of age are kept, during long weary days, seated with a large lace-pillow on their knees, leaning over their work, the chest doubled, and toiling without a rest. Many of these young laborers here contract the germ of a fatal malady. Happily the progress of industry and modern invention has dealt this trade a heavy blow and it is slowly disappearing from the number of female occupations. Some years ago it was not uncommon to see, in the streets of our country villages, poor women, who had been brought up in the convents, busy at lace-making before daybreak in order to gain their bread. At present the pay is so small that it does not suffice to support them, and the industry is now limited almost wholly to religious establishments.

Such a situation, like that of the employment of women

and children in factories and mines, demands energetic protective measures. But that this reform may be radical and produce all the fruits legitimately expected, it should be combined with a law rendering instruction obligatory.

If we mount a round higher in the social ladder, we meet with the woman of the lower middle class, *la petite bourgeoisie*. Although she is not the slave of the factory, she is an industrious worker, has a calling, keeps store, exercises a trade. Often by her activity, her labor, her strong will, her real genius for order and economy, she becomes, more than man, the bread-winner and support of the family. She nourishes love of home and transmits to the children the ideas of duty and virtue. Possessing some instruction herself, she endeavors to develop their minds. The father is busy with his occupations far from home, and in the hours of repose seeks for amusement outside of the family circle. The mother is more with the children; she brings them up and is their guide. And yet this woman, often the real head of the family, is kept by the law in a condition of perpetual tutelage. But I need not dwell upon the general question of how the married woman is treated by the Napoleonic code; the subject is too well known.* One point, however, which has struck me most painfully, I would briefly touch upon here. The code takes great care to save the fortune of the wife when it is endangered by the prodigality of the husband : when her dower is in peril, she may demand a " separation of goods " (*séparation de biens*). But in order to ask for this separation, the wife must have a dower (*dot*); in other words, she must belong

---

* See the chapter on France, where this topic is ably handled by M. Léon Giraud.—T. S.

at the moment of the marriage, to a well-to-do family, which can bestow on her a dower. The code has entirely overlooked the poor wife, who, by her own industry, has slowly acquired a little sum. What protection does the law afford her against the prodigality and dissipation of the husband? None whatever. The separation of goods —whether there be a dower or not—would frequently be a blessing to many families. Under the present law, a husband may dissipate in a single day the hard earnings of a long life-time, without the wife being able to lift a finger in her own defence. Is this not a sovereign injustice?

And what will-power, energy and tenacity of purpose women must have in Belgium, as elsewhere, in order to secure a little footing in the world! Women's work is very poorly paid. The larger number, if not all, of employments, trades, and professions are monopolized by men. Women are generally considered incapable of doing anything. The example of other countries, however, has modified this situation, and the liberal spirit of our government has removed barriers which shut women out from certain employments. A good beginning has been made. In certain cities of Belgium, women are admitted to the postal and telegraphic service. But the circle of their activity should be enlarged, so that a greater number might have the means of procuring an honorable and independent position. Let us hope that the advantages already obtained will encourage further progress in the same direction.

To give women work is to save them not only from starvation but from vice. Recent lawsuits, the discussions of the press, and various publications, notably those of the Brussels Society of Public Morality (*Société de moral-*

ité publique*), have revealed misery and shame which would never have been suspected. A woman who has once fallen finds herself, under the *régime* of legalized prostitution which exists in Belgium, in such a position that it is almost impossible for her to break from her chains. That noble woman, Mrs. Josephine E. Butler, well said at Neufchatel: " This modern slavery, with its train of atrocities, is an outrage, not only on women, but on all humanity ;" and M. Emile de Laveleye, the eminent Belgian publicist, has also remarked: " Persons object to the State charging itself with the instruction of the people, and deny still more strongly its right to protect women against excessive labor which destroys their health, and yet these same persons tolerate the State enrolling women by force in the ranks of the army of legalized debauchery." The legalization of vice appears to me to be such an odious thing, and the powers put in the hands of the police are so excessive, that I cannot understand how the abuse, once pointed out, is suffered to continue.

Mounting one more round of the social ladder, we reach the opulent commoner, or *bourgeoise*, and the aristocratic lady. Although these women form two very distinct classes in society, meeting but never mingling, the instruction and education which they receive and the influence which they exercise in their respective centres, are very much the same. I think I may say that, with few exceptions, this influence is null, and may be taken as the measure of the moral and intellectual development of

---

* This society is the representative in Belgium of Mrs. Butler's association for the abolition of legalized prostitution. Its secretary is the liberal-minded publicist, M. Jules Pagny, of Saventhem, and its president, the distinguished professor of Liege, M. Emile de Laveleye.—I. van D.

these women. We find here no brutalizing toil, no precarious existence, no worry about the daily bread, which fetters body and mind and checks the proper development of both. But, while difficulties which embarrass the upper classes are not the same as those with which the poor are forced to contend, they are none the less disastrous, and greatly modify the advantages of position and fortune, which might make it possible for the girl and wife to become strong, original individualities, capable of understanding their mission and of fulfilling it intelligently. The daughters of the fashionable world are early seized upon by the convents. The religious sisters, whose duty it is to instruct and prepare these young girls for the existence awaiting them outside of the cloister walls, have no idea, or at least a very wrong one, of real life, which they know only through the medium of exaggerated or false narratives, or the dim recollections of their youth. The sentimental and imaginative faculties are abnormally developed, to the utter neglect of sound reason and the practical things of this earth ; and in this condition they are taken from their seclusion and launched into society. Provided with a very poor stock of knowledge, some precepts of conduct which they never find means of applying, and with a few accomplishments, they give themselves up to a round of *fêtes* and pleasures, until the object to be accomplished—finding a husband—is attained. If the girl is not very attractive, if wanting in energy, or if her education has destroyed what little she ever had, she will accept the first man who presents himself fulfilling the conditions required by her family, and from parental tutelage will pass to that of her husband, doomed to live and die a perpetual minor. But if perchance she wakes up one day to a full consciousness of her position, and perceives the extent of her misfortune, how this existence which she has thoughtlessly accepted weighs upon her! She will revolt perhaps, seek amusement and endeavor to find some compensation for her painful lot, unless the grand duties of maternity come to sustain her, to console her and to fill the void in her heart.

Thus, following different routes, we find at both ends of the social ladder the same result : woman's intelligence neglected and left in a state of infancy. I fear it will be a long time, if we may judge by the present condition of things, before our Belgian girls, in imitation of their aristocratic sisters of England, will themselves rise up and assume as high a rank in the intellectual sphere as that which they hold in the social world.

A word remains to be said concerning the admission of women to the walks of higher education, and notably to the study of medicine. There existed in Belgium some years ago a law which required students who would enter the university, to pass the examination of graduate in letters (*gradué en lettres*.) Candidates for this degree were expected to know how to translate Greek and write Latin. But as there were no schools where girls could study the dead languages with the thoroughness of boys, who were trained six years in the classics, the former were almost entirely shut out from enjoying the advantages of an university course. This *graduat*, however, no longer exists, and the entrance of women into our universities is now possible. Female students are found to-day at Brussels, Liege and Ghent, but their number is still very small. It was in 1880 that the first woman entered the university of Brussels, but it was not until 1883 that their admission became general. They pursue, for the most part scientific studies, thereby securing more lucrative positions as teachers, and pass their examinations for graduation with success. The higher education of women is still an open question in Belgium, and there are those who oppose it. But the experience of Switzerland, England and France, not to mention other countries on both sides of the Atlantic, answers victoriously all objections. And does not the long list of the world's distinguished women prove that the female sex is capable of the highest intellectual culture? Not to go outside of belles-lettres, and the limits of Belgium, we have Miss Nizet, Marguerite Van de Wiele, the Countess de Kerchove de Denterghem, the Loveling sisters, Mrs. Courtmans, Mrs. Van Ackere, and many others.*

The progress of modern ideas tends to destroy day by day the prejudices which still exist in Belgium against the emancipation of women. We are far from the time when woman was a slave and grave bishops in council doubted whether she had a soul. Let us hope that the age is past when woman can be left in ignorance, and that soon the means will be no longer lacking by which she can elevate herself to the intellectual level of the other sex. Then will Belgium enjoy all the other reforms, and woman will become the equal of man in every department of life.

---

* Mr. Emile de Laveleye, writing me from the university of Liege in January, 1883, said: "Our female students have not yet taken their degrees. But as they are working very hard, I have no doubt they will be successful. But co-education will not be so exempt from danger here as in America. Our morals are very inferior to yours." Mr. de Laveleye, in an interesting little pamphlet entitled, "University Education for Women" (*L'instruction supérieure pour les femmes*, Bruxelles, Librairie Européenne, 1882), gives an account of the movement in favor of female instruction in Belgium. These pages show that many of our American Universities could learn lessons in liberality from their sister institutions of Belgium.—T. S.

CHAPTER III

GERMANY.

I. A GENERAL REVIEW OF THE WOMEN'S MOVEMENT IN GERMANY.

BY ANNA SCHEPELER-LETTE AND JENNY HIRSCH.

[Mrs. Anna Schepeler-Lette was born December 19, 1829, at Soldin, Germany, and was the eldest daughter of Dr. Lette—mentioned in the following pages—whom she accompanied, in 1848, to Frankfort-on-the-Main, whither he went as a member of the German Parliament. In 1866 she joined her father at Berlin, and was initiated into the work of the Lette Society, to which admirable organization she has ever since devoted all her time and energy. Mrs. Schepeler-Lette went to America in 1876, and visited the Centennial Exhibition, and many of the principal cities of the United States, where she carefully examined various institutions whose aims were similar to those of the Lette Society.

Miss Jenny Hirsch, born November 25, 1829, at Zerbst, Germany, was brought up as a child by very strictly orthodox Jewish parents, but, although she had many narrow prejudices to contend against, secured by her own efforts a good education. In 1860 Miss Hirsch went to Berlin, became interested in a fashion paper, and accumulated in four years sufficient money to enable her to devote herself entirely to literary work. At this epoch she published numerous essays and criticisms, and many translations from the French, English, and Swedish, among others John Stuart Mill's " Subjection of Women." Since the spring of 1866 Miss Hirsch has been the secretary of the Lette Society and editor of the *German Women's Advocate* (*Deutscher Frauen-Anwalt*), which is devoted to the industrial and general education of women.]

THE woman question, like several other ideas thrust

99

upon the attention of the world by the French Revolution, was not hastily accepted by the German mind. Many excellent reforms have encountered a long and obstinate resistance on this side of the Rhine simply because they were said to be a product of the upheaval of 1789, and the women's movement, in addition to its unfortunate origin, was brought into disrepute as the " Emancipation of Women." The greatest stumbling-block in our way has been the signification given to this term, and we tacitly agreed to avoid its use, although it was impossible to find one which could exactly replace it.

The year 1848 was the signal for the setting free of forces until then held in check, and new truths were propagated of which the masses had scarcely a presentiment a few days before. It was the early spring time in the life of nations. It produced a forced and quick growth, and its effect was felt even by women. Mrs. Louise Otto-Peters, of Leipsic, who has since become well-known, caught the spirit of the times, proclaimed the principle of women's progress, and devoted her great energies and talents to the young cause.

The brilliant beginnings and lofty hopes of 1848 were immediately followed by a sombre and troubled period. The liberty trees were planted in a soil so poor and badly prepared that they could not take root. They soon perished under the influence of the reaction which set in, and all that had been accomplished for good or for evil in that short season was indiscriminately destroyed. What had been done for the amelioration of the condition of women shared the common fate. For the moment these questions were forgotten ; they were pushed aside, repressed, but they could not be extirpated. Political and social life could no longer be confined within the narrow limits which had existed previous to the Revolution of 1848. The woman question also came to the surface again, and in 1865 we find it once more before the public, when it took on the form by which it has since been known, marching on, year after year, from victory to victory.

The most striking proof of the vitality and the necessity of the reformation lay in the fact that it was demanded at the same time in various places, so that its advocates, ignorant of each other, differed on minor points. The woman question in Germany has this same argument in its favor; it sprang up simultaneously in several parts of the country, and especially at Leipsic and Berlin.

The Leipsic movement had its origin in a women's meeting—to which men, however, were admitted—held in that city in October, 1865, and due to the efforts of Mrs. Louise Otto-Peters, of whom we have already spoken. The Berlin movement dates from a gathering of both sexes at the capital in December of the same year, under the presidency of Dr. Adolf Lette, one of the most eminent philanthropists Germany has produced. At Leipsic, where the feminine element predominated, the question was regarded rather from the standpoint of sentiment, while at Berlin, where business men took part, more practical measures were adopted. In both places, however, good sense prevailed, and all felt that in order to construct a solid and durable edifice the foundation must be made before the roof, that slow and conservative, rather than hasty and radical, steps would be better in the end.

The first meeting in Berlin was followed in February of the next year, 1866, by the foundation of the Society for the Promotion of the Employment of Women (*Verein zur*

Förderung der Erwerbsfähigkeit des weiblichen Geschlechts). The new organization was placed under the patronage of the Crown Princess, and in 1869 its name was changed to the Lette Society (*Lette-Verein*) in honor of its founder, who died December 3, 1868.

Fault is sometimes found because the movement has been separated into two currents ever since its beginning. There is unquestionably much ground for this criticism, and we do not deny that our efforts would have produced more fruit if both organizations had worked together. But here comes into play a peculiarity of the German character which has considerably modified the evil. The two associations, although occasionally at variance, have not acted to the detriment of the common cause, but, on the contrary, they have displayed greater zeal, and have more quickly discovered and corrected errors, because of their independent positions.

The chief aim of the Leipsic reformers, the National Association of German Women (*Der allgemeine deutsche Frauen-Verein*), was to produce a broad and thorough agitation of the general question of women's rights, while in Berlin the object in view was more immediate, precise and limited. The former strove to disseminate the new ideas, and, for this purpose, annual congresses or conventions were held in different parts of the country, where eloquent addresses were delivered by these pioneers, and local societies established.

Although the Lette Society was not founded for the purpose of propagandism, this important agency is not excluded from its plan of work. The scope of the organization was clearly set forth in an essay, read by Dr. Lette before the Central Society for the Improvement of the Working

Classes of Prussia (*Central-Verein für das Wohl der arbeitenden Klassen in Preussen*), in which he proved, by the aid of statistics, that a large body of women were forced to earn their own livelihood, and that marriage—since females outnumbered males in Prussia, and also because of certain economic reasons—was not always possible. He called attention to the precarious situation of the daughters of poor government employes when, on the death of their father, they are thrown upon the world wholly unprepared for the struggle of life. He spoke of the few pursuits open to women, of the over-crowding of those not shut against them, and of the low pay resulting from this state of things; and, in conclusion, he predicted fatal results if the sphere of their activity was not enlarged and employments which were once theirs were not restored to them.

These ideas formed the basis of the Lette Society, whose organization was substantially that of the London Society for Promoting the Employment of Women. We did not, however, servilely follow the English model, but while we utilized the experiences of the London Society, we did not hesitate to introduce modifications demanded by the peculiarities of the German character. The essential principles and aims of the Lette Society have been, from the beginning, to discover new occupations fitted for women, to protect their interests in those where they already have a footing, and to educate them for more important and profitable employments.

Notwithstanding the many difficulties which the society has encountered during its long period of activity, it has, on the whole, remained faithful to its origin. It is true that we have found it more and more necessary to devote attention to practical instruction, for it was soon discovered that most women did not know how to work carefully, conscientiously, and accurately. This is not due, however, to any innate and fundamental defect in the sex, but is rather a result of bad education and habits, which, as experience has shown, quickly disappear, and are replaced by remarkable aptitude as soon as irregular employment gives place to methodical work preceded by a rational preparation.

After the death of its founder and first president, the Lette Society was directed for several years by Dr. von Holtzendorf, professor at the University of Berlin, until Mrs. Schepeler-Lette succeeded to the post in 1872, where she has ever since remained.

The society supports at this moment, at its rooms in Königgrätzer Strasse, Berlin, a commercial school, a drawing and modeling school, and a cooking school, while it also gives instruction in washing, ironing, cutting, dressmaking, hand and machine sewing, the manufacture of artificial flowers, and many other kinds of manual and art work. The pupils of these various schools are prepared for the State examinations for drawing teachers and instructors in mechanic arts, and subsequently find employment in boarding, private, and girls' grammar schools. In another building is a printing office, where women are taught to set type. The society also conducts a boarding-house for women (*Das Victoriastift*), and in connection with it a women's restaurant. A shop for the sale of female handiwork, known as the Victoria Bazaar, a free intelligence office, and a bank where women may make on easy terms small loans, with which to commence or enlarge their business, or to buy sewing machines, are some of the other admirable features of the Lette Society.

The number of those who have been benefited by this institution can be counted by the thousands, so that a great and good work has been accomplished with proportionally very small means. Nor has its usefulness been limited to the capital alone. The reputation of the society has spread throughout the country, and similar organizations have been established in Bremen, Hamburg, Breslau, Brunswick, Rostock, Stettin, and Potsdam. At Darmstadt is the Alice Society (*Alice-Verein*), devoted to the industrial and general instruction of women, and whose patroness was Alice, the late Grand Duchess of Hesse. There are like institutions at Dusseldorf, Cologne, Elberfeld, Weisbaden, Königsberg, Dantsic, and other cities, all modeled after the Lette Society, whence are drawn their corps of teachers. The societies founded by the National Association of German Women, as well as those which have sprung up independently of both organizations, are all working in the same field, have a similar aim in view, and are animated by that spirit of moderation which has done so much for the success of the common cause.

It cannot be said of this movement that it purposes to overthrow existing institutions, that it desires to estrange women from their peculiar vocation in the family, State, and society. This conservative character of the German reformers has been criticised. They have been found too timid, too considerate of old prejudices, too slow, too circumspect. The stricture arises mainly, however, from an imperfect understanding of the situation in this country. Because of the excellent system of compulsory education which exists in Germany, we had not to begin so low down as in some other parts of Europe. All German girls were furnished with, at least, the foundation of an education. And yet the women's movement has accomplished admirable reforms in this very field. To it is due the introduction into the girls' primary schools (*Volksschule*) of compulsory and systematic instruction in sewing and similar handiwork, and the persevering and finally successful efforts to enlarge the scope of the girls' grammar schools (*Töchterschule*), efforts which have met with the approval of competent persons and which have not passed unnoticed by the government itself. Still greater progress might be made in this direction, if only the proper laws were enacted. All attempts to bring about the establishment by the municipalities or the government of girls' high schools have failed, but it is almost beyond doubt that this worthy object will be accomplished sooner or later. When it is, women will be able to obtain a training similar to that furnished at the boys' gymnasiums, so that, provided with a diploma (*Abiturientenzeugniss*) they may enter the universities and receive a degree.

German women who would secure a higher education must study in private, for their admission into the lecture-rooms of any of our universities is very difficult. Female students, to our knowledge, have been admitted only at Heidelberg and Leipsic, and even in these two institutions they have not been suffered to pass the examinations. It is at foreign universities that our women are forced to pursue their studies and take their degrees. The two female physicians at Berlin, Dr. Franziska Tiburtius, and Dr. Emilie Lehmus, are graduates of Zurich, and Lina Beger, Ph. D., who began her career as a teacher at the capital, received her degree at Bern. The two Berlin dentists, Mrs. Dr. Tiburtius Hirschfeldt, and Miss Carsten, studied at Philadelphia.

In its treatment of the great question of the higher education of women, Germany is outstripped, not only by the republics of Switzerland, America and France, but lags behind the monarchies of England, Sweden, Italy, and Russia, which, after an obstinate resistance, have finally opened their universities to women and graduated them with full academic honors. We are convinced that Germany must soon follow their example, either by the foundation of special institutions or by throwing wide the doors of the existing universities. But we fear that the struggle will be longer and harder here than in other countries, for our universities, venerable by their antiquity and conservative by their organization, are immutable for good or evil. The same thing is seen in England, where the London University, which is of recent origin, long ago conferred its advantages on women, while ancient Cambridge and Oxford, although they have made some concessions, still hold back.*

Until that day arrives, we must be contented with those excellent institutions which have sprung up in many cities under the name of lyceums (*Lyceen*) and which afford our girls admirable instruction.† The oldest and best known

---

* The United States presents similar examples. While Cornell, Michigan, and other young universities are not afraid of women, venerable Harvard, Yale and Columbia, the latter in spite of the repeated efforts of President Barnard in favor of the reform, tremble for their future if co-education be adopted.—T. S.

† The prospectus of the Victoria Lyceum at Cologne, of which Mrs. Lina Schneider, a lady of wide culture, is the principal, gives a fair idea of the scope of these institutions. " The instruction comprises," says this prospectus, " thorough English in all its branches, German, French, Italian (taught respectively by native professors), Latin and Greek classics, mathematics, shorthand-writing, history, literature, and other sciences, music, drawing, painting, calisthenics, and all female accomplishments. * * *

of these educational establishments is the Victoria Lyceum, in Berlin, founded and directed by Miss Archer. It
contains the nuclei of what could be developed on the one
hand into a gymnasium, and on the other into a university. The Alice Lyceum, established at Darmstadt by
Louise Büchner, would have attained an equally high
position if its growth had not been suddenly checked by
the death of its founder, who, as Vice-president of the
Alice Society, and as a writer on the woman question,
showed marked ability and accomplished much good
work. Lyceums patterned after these two have been
organized at Breslau, Karlsruhe, Dresden, Cologne, and
Leipsic.

Closely connected with this movement in favor of the
higher education of women and of the amelioration of
their position in the field of labor, is the effort to spread
the Fröbel system. Many of the industrial societies
(*Erwerbvereine*) already mentioned have accepted Fröbel's
ideas, and have opened kindergarten schools, courses
for the instruction of teachers for such schools, and
courses for the preparation of children's nurses. Nobody interested in the general progress of women can un-
derrate this important work, and Mrs. Johanna Gold-
schmidt, of Hamburg, a pioneer of the Fröbel system, will
always occupy an honorable place among those who have
labored in this field.

Women's domestic duties are not excluded from the
programme of our movement. Hygiene, the care of chil-

There are also opportunities for learning dancing, swimming, skating, and
riding." It appears that the lyceum can prepare (the prospectus from which
I quote is addressed to the English public) " with special facility and success for the Oxford and Cambridge local, the Irish intermediate, the University or other examinations."—T. S.

dren and rational housekeeping are essential parts of any plan of female education. Furthermore, women should know how to care for the sick of their own household, and should even be taught professional nursing. There may be a question as to whether they should be physicians, but as regards the training of women as nurses there can be but one opinion. The Catholic and Protestant Churches have long had training schools for nurses, and similar institutions have sprung up all over the country during the past fifteen years. The oldest of them is the Baden Women's Society (*Badischer Frauen-Verein*), under the protection of the Grand Duchess Louise, which has many branches, and which, besides the instruction of nurses, succors the poor and aids working women.

The Women's Patriotic Society (*Vaterländischer Frauen-Verein*), patronized by the Empress, besides doing a work similar to that of the last mentioned organization, in time of war takes care of the families of militiamen (*Landwehr*) in service, establishes hospitals, nurses the wounded, etc. The same ground is covered by the Albert Society (*Albert-Verein*) in Saxony, to which the regretted Marie Simon devoted her life; the Olga Society (*Olga-Verein*) in Würtemberg, which is patronized by the good Queen Olga, and by like bodies in Bavaria, Saxe-Weimar, Mecklenburg, etc.

Three groups of women's associations still remain to be mentioned. The German Teachers' and Governesses' Society (*Verein deutscher Lehrerinenen und Erzieherinenen*), which, with its branches, looks after the intellectual and material interests of teachers, possesses in the neighborhood of Berlin a retreat for aged and invalid members of the profession. It has also organized boarding houses and clubs, where male and female teachers meet to discuss subjects which interest them. The second group consists of Housekeepers' Societies (*Hausfrauen-Vereine*), which owe their origin to Mrs. Lina Morgenstern, to whom is also due the Soup-kitchens (*Volksküchen*), where the poor are fed at a very moderate price. All the important questions pertaining to domestic economy, come within the scope of these excellent associations. The third and last group are Societies of Art Students (*Vereine der Kunstlerinnen*), which, as is the case at Berlin, have established schools where women may study painting and sculpture; it being difficult, if not absolutely impossible, for them to obtain admission to the School of Fine Arts. There are similar institutions for women at Weimar and Munich, though the school in the latter city is more especially devoted to industrial art, while many pursue their studies in the studios of eminent artists.

Our women have proved by their productions that they have richly profited by these advantages. The last two exhibitions of fine arts at Berlin, and the international exhibition at Munich, in 1879, contained specimens of female talent which received the highest praise from impartial critics. It is no exaggeration to say that women contribute in no small degree to the art industry of Germany. With the needle, the pencil, the brush, they produce magnificent ornamental work. The schools of art and design established by the Berlin Industrial Museum (*Gewerbe-Museum*) and the Lette Society, and the similar institutions in Munich, Reutlingen, Karlsruhe, Dresden, and other cities, have turned out many trained women who have become teachers or artificers of fine needlework, designers, pattern-makers, and the like.

German unity, so long desired and so heartily welcomed, has been prejudicial, we are sorry to say, to the employment of women, as in Austria, in the railroad, postal, and telegraphic service. While the States of South and Central Germany have long availed themselves of females for these positions, Prussia and the countries united with her in the postal and telegraphic union have taken the opposite course. When, on the formation of the Empire, the government assumed control of the post-office and telegraph, it looked for a moment as if all the female employes would be dismissed. A petition, however, was sent to the Imperial Parliament (*Reichstag*) in 1872, which not only checked this tendency, but secured the admission of women into the telegraphic and postal service of Prussia itself. But, as the Postmaster General of Germany, Mr. Stephan, is opposed to the employment of women in his department, everything has been done to defeat the measure, so that we are forced to admit that in this matter our country has taken a step backward.*

But, on the whole, the agitation begun at Leipsic and Berlin, has accomplished a great deal during the past eighteen years. We have been able to give here only an incomplete outline of its history. What has been written in Germany, for and against the woman question, would form a large library. A number of periodicals are exclusively devoted to this subject. Besides the *New Paths* (*Neue Bahnen*), the organ of the Leipsic movement, we may cite housekeepers' journals published at Berlin and Cologne, also a paper which represents the interests of

---

* Mr. Stephan's course is strongly contrasted by that of the English Post-master General, and is a striking example of how much the success of laws, even under the modern parliamentary *régime*, depends upon the personal opinions of those who execute them. For an account of what Mr. Fawcett and others have done in England in connection with this subject, see page 93.—T. S.

girls' high schools, and the *German Women's Advocate* (*Deutscher Frauen-Anwalt*), organ of the United Societies for the Education and Employment of Women (*Verband des deutscher Frauenbildungs und Erwerbvereine*).

The last named organization was formed in November, 1869, at a meeting in Berlin of delegates from all parts of Germany, and embraces a large number of women's industrial, educational, house-keeping and Fröbel societies, and training schools for nurses. It holds general meetings at irregular intervals. Such assemblies have occurred at Darmstadt, Hamburg, Weisbaden, and at Berlin, in the autumn of 1879, where delegates were present from the Leipsic National Society. At these congresses all the various themes relating to women are discussed; resolutions are passed, subjects for prize-essays announced, and petitions sent to the Government. At the Berlin Congress petitions were drawn up praying for the admission of women into the pharmaceutical profession, for the providing of means for their higher education, for their employment in the postal and telegraphic service, and for the modification of certain regulations which check their participation in business and trade.

More radical demands than these have not been seriously made in Germany. The opening of politics to women has not been pressed. Contrary to the course pursued by the American and English reformers, who hold that the only way to emancipate the sex is by means of the electoral franchise, and who consequently make suffrage the chief aim of all their efforts, we Germans believe that the lever is found in education. In working for the present generation, and in helping women already half through the journey of life to earn their daily bread, we are sowing seed which will bear a rich fruitage in the future. Thanks to our untiring labors the conviction is spreading that every woman, rich or poor, high or low, ought to have an education such as will make her, in the highest and best sense, the helpmate and companion of man—wife, mother, and teacher. The German movement aims to elevate the whole female sex, and to render women capable of serving themselves, the family, society, the State, and humanity. Our object is to lift women out of their insignificance, frivolity, poverty, misery, and shame, and train them for work which will render themselves and others happy, and thus advance the general interests of civilization.

II. THE NATIONAL ASSOCIATION OF GERMAN WOMEN.

BY MARIE CALM.

[Miss Marie Calm was born at Arolsen (where her father was burgomaster or mayor), in the Principality of Waldeck, on April 3, 1832. She was sent to a private school in her native town and finished her education at a well-known boarding school in Geneva, where she made great progress in the English and French languages. Afterward Miss Calm spent three years in England and two years in Russia, returning to Germany to take charge of a girls' high school in the Rhenish Provinces.. Her first appearance in literature was as a story writer in the noted *Illustrated World* (*Illustrirte Welt*) of Stuttgart. In 1865 she heard of the movement in Leipsic in favor of women—which she describes in the following pages, put herself in communication with the leaders of the new agitation and was invited by them to take part in their next congress. She accepted this invitation in 1867, and has ever since been one of the most zealous advocates of women's rights in Germany. At Cassel, where she now resides, Miss Calm has done much for the education of girls by opening, in conjunction with some other ladies, an industrial school which has proved most successful. Since 1869 she has lectured all over Germany on educational subjects, has founded girls' schools similar to that at Cassel and organized women's societies auxiliary to the National

Association. Miss Calm is the author of stories, poems, works on pedagogics, and "Leo," a novel in three volumes, "which fastens the reader's attention with the first page," says an American writer, "and holds it unwaveringly to the closing paragraph." I had the pleasure of making Miss Calm's acquaintance at Paris in 1881, and was struck not only by her excellent command of English and French, both of which languages she speaks and writes with great ease, but also by her agreeable presence, her enthusiasm and her liberalism.]

THE National Association of German Women (*Der allgemeine deutsche Frauen-Verein*), was founded at Leipsic in October, 1865, and was the first organized movement in Germany in favor of what is now known as the Woman Question (*Frauenfrage*). I do not wish to say that previous to this date many noble minds had not examined the great subject of women's needs and women's position, but what I do mean is that until the autumn of 1865 this work had been isolated, unorganized and consequently barren of practical results. Again, the few women who, about fifty years ago, tried to cut free from the restraints imposed upon their sex and to gain the liberty denied them by society, overstepped the limits of what is considered womanly by imitating the other sex in dress, in smoking, etc., so that the word *emancipation*, originally applied to their agitation, has ever since retained an odious meaning and is therefore carefully discarded by the leaders of the present movement.

This latter movement is indeed quite different in its origin, its aims and its means from the generous, but rather sentimental, outburst of 1830. The English census of 1856 had brought to light the fact that two millions of women in that country were dependent upon their own labor for their livelihood, and that most of them knew not how to work, or were so poorly paid that, as the German saying goes, they had too much to die, too little to

114

live. About this time Hood's "Song of the Shirt" appeared in all our newspapers, rousing the public to indignation at the neglected condition of working women and filling it with pity for the unhappy creature of whom the poet sang. A census in Prussia shortly afterward proved that there was about the same number of women in that country who were unprovided for, and drew attention to the crying necessity of giving them the means of earning their daily bread. Some philanthropists wrote and spoke on the subject, and Dr. Adolph Lette, a man of eminent merit, gave permanent form to this new public sentiment by establishing what afterward became the admirable Lette Society.

Among the women who, not only then but long before, had shown a deep interest in the amelioration of the condition of her sex, stands in the front rank, Mrs. Louise Otto-Peters. In her novels, most of which treat social questions, she has always pleaded for the oppressed, and when, after the publication of her "Castle and Factory" (*Schloss und Fabrik*), a deputation of Leipsic workmen invited her to contribute to their newspaper, she replied that she would gladly do so if allowed to defend the cause of work-women in its columns. She also took a very active part in the political movement of 1848, and founded in that year the first women's paper, to my knowledge, in Germany, which bore the motto "I enlist women in the cause of liberty" (*Dem Reich der Freiheit werb' ich Bürgerinnen*). The reactionary period which followed put an end to the paper, but Louise Otto continued fearlessly devoted to woman and liberty.

It was very natural, therefore, that she should become

the centre of a movement for promoting the welfare of her sex. In October, 1865, a few men and women met in Leipsic to consider the subject, and the conference ended, as has already been said, in the foundation of the National Association of German·Women. The name was rather ambitious when we consider the small number of persons who were present at the birth of the organization. But they looked far into the future, and ardently trusted that in the course of time the title of their young creation would be no misnomer. The Association set itself the task of elevating the educational and social position of one half of the nation. It declared work to be the right, the duty and the honor of women as well as of men, and denounced all those obstacles which hinder the former from a free participation in every employment and profession for which they are fitted by nature. In order to propagate these ideas it was resolved to establish a newspaper and to hold annual conventions in different parts of Germany.

The organ of the Association, a bi-monthly, which treats all aspects of the woman question, both in Europe and America, was named *New Paths* (*Neue Bahnen*), and has been edited from the beginning by Mrs. Louise Otto Peters and her friend, Miss Auguste Schmidt. But reforms are not accomplished by the pen alone. Our articles are read chiefly by those already friendly to our views, not by our opponents, and least of all by the great mass of the indifferent. It therefore appeared necessary for the complete success of the cause to propagate it by word of mouth. Never had women assembled in Germany to discuss their own position in society; never had they been seen on the platform addressing an audience with eloquence and logic. These were prerogatives of the masculine sex alone. The National Association of German Women was first to show that the other sex, too, was capable and ready to present its claims before the public. But our aim was not simply to be heard, but to convince; and this object has always been attained. Wherever our congresses have been held, we have met with success, as witness those of Leipsic (1867 and 1871), that of Brunswick (1868), Cassel (1869), Eisenach (1872), Stuttgart (1873), Gotha (1875), Frankfort-on-the-Main (1876), Hanover (1877), Heidelberg (1879) and Lübeck (1881). * These meetings have, of course, encountered strong prejudices. People were curious to hear what women had to say; they wished only to be amused, but many became interested, convinced, and often before the close of the sessions were enthusiastic supporters of the cause.

In these congresses addresses are delivered on all subjects connected with the woman question, and reports are read by delegates of the work accomplished by the auxiliary societies, so that the audience obtains a pretty good idea of the operations of the National Association since the previous meeting.† At the end of each congress an

---

* In a recent letter from Miss Calm, she says : " There has not been any congress this (1882) year, owing to the Berlin Society being rather loath to undertake the trouble and cost of these meetings. It was their turn and they postponed it. I am going to Leipsic next week in order to arrange with my colleagues about next year's congress."—T. S.

† The following programme of the last congress, will give the best idea of the nature of these assemblages, and of the scope of the National Association.

THE ELEVENTH CONGRESS OF THE NATIONAL ASSOCIATION
OF GERMAN WOMEN,
HELD AT LÜBECK FROM THE 5TH TO THE 6TH OF OCTOBER, 1881.

Wednesday, Oct. 5th, 10 A.M.—Business meeting. Election of officers, etc. 7 P.M.—First public session. Reception of the delegates by the local committee. Preliminary addresses by Miss Auguste Schmidt, of Leipsic.

effort is made to found a local auxiliary society (*Lokal-Verein*), which accepts the plan of the National Association and endeavors to embody its aims in some useful institution. Organizations of this kind have thus been established in all the above-mentioned cities with one exception, and in several other places through the efforts of individuals. They have created girls' industrial or professional schools, mercantile institutes and lyceums. In some instances the members of these societies arrange courses of lectures and hold monthly gatherings, where women of all classes meet on a common footing, either to listen to an essay, to discuss subjects of mutual interest, or to be diverted by music and declamation. Similar entertainments are sometimes offered to working-women, who thus enjoy simple and innocent amusements.

Since the year 1876 an agreement has existed between the National Association and the United Societies, at the head of which stands the Lette Society, for calling these congresses alternately, and for sending delegates from the one organization to the congress held under the auspices of the other. But the spirit of active propagandism and

---

Thursday, Oct. 6th, 10 A.M.—Business meeting. Treasurer's report, etc. 3 P.M. to 5 P.M.—Visit to the churches and other celebrated monuments of the city. 6 P.M.—Second public session. Opening of the Congress by Mrs. Louise Otto-Peters, of Leipsic. Address by Miss Marie Calm, of Cassel, on "The Women's Movement in its Principal Localities from a Historical Point of View." Reports of delegates. Address by Miss Willborn, of Schwerin, on "The Scientific Education of Female Teachers." Social reunion. Friday, Oct. 7th, 9 A.M.—Third session. Address by Miss Menzzer, of Dresden, on "The Compensation of Women's Labor." Reports. Address by Miss Assmann, of Hanover, on "The Citizenship of Women." 3 P.M.—Address by Mrs. Füllgraff, M.D., of Hamburg, on "Women's Position in America." Reports. Address by Mrs. Lina Morgenstern, of Berlin, on "The Food Question." 7 P.M.—Banquet.—M. C.

the foundation of new societies appear to be alone pecu‑
liar to the congresses of the National Association.

In 1877 the executive committee of the Association
sent to the Imperial Parliament (*Reichstag*) a petition
signed by a great number of women, praying for certain
of their civil rights, for the amelioration of their condition
as wives and mothers, and for the abrogation of those laws
which treat them as minors. This petition was accom‑
panied by a memorial, drawn up by Louise Otto‑Peters,
which contained all the laws concerning women as found
in the different statute books of Germany, for it must be
borne in mind that every State, and even a great many
towns, of the Empire has a code of its own. The answer
of Parliament to this petition was that a code common to
all Germany was soon to be prepared, and that then our
demands should be considered.*

The above‑mentioned executive committee consists of
Mrs. Louise Otto‑Peters, Miss Auguste Schmidt, the as‑
sociate editor of the *Neue Bahnen* and one of the ablest
speakers in our congresses; and Mrs. Henriette Gold‑

---

* I select a few paragraphs from the Prussian and Bavarian codes. *Ex uno
disce omnes.* Here is the law of Prussia : Children may not marry without
the consent of the father.—§45. (So the mother is of no account when it
comes to giving up her daughter !) By marriage the husband obtains con‑
trol of the wife's fortune.—§205. Whatever the wife earns during her mar‑
riage belongs to the husband.—§211. The wife may not contract any debts on
the fortune she has brought to the husband.—§§318 and 319. (He has the
right to squander the whole of it, but she may not spend a farthing of what
was once her own !) In regard to divorce : Bodily ill treatment may be a
cause of divorce, if it endangers the health or life of the wife (!).—§685. Here
are a few specimens from the Bavarian statute‑book : By marriage the wife
comes under the authority of the husband and the law (*Gewalt*) allows him
to chastise her moderately (!).—§2. Women, with the exception of the mother
and grandmother, are unfit to be guardians.—§90. (So are minors, lunatics,
and spendthrifts !)—M. C.

schmidt, a leading promoter of the Fröbel system in Germany, who has formed a society in Leipsic for popular education and a girls' lyceum, and who, by her eloquence and her lectures in different parts of the country, has done a great deal to keep alive public interest in the various phases of the woman question. These three ladies and Mrs. Winter, treasurer of the Association, live in Leipsic. Another member of the committee, Miss Menzzer, is at the head of a Women's Educational Society (*Frauenbildungs Verein*) at Dresden; a sixth, Mrs. Lina Morgenstern, is a lady of great talent and activity; and, lastly, the writer of this sketch, who is president of the Women's Educational Society of Cassel.

This brief account shows that the National Association of German Women has not been unsuccessful in its efforts to raise the level of instruction and thereby to improve the general condition of the sex. It is to be hoped that the interest in this question may spread wider and wider —and it was for the accomplishment of this end that our Association was founded—until the victory is complete, and women secure in the family and in the State the position to which they are entitled, but which customs and laws so often deny them.

CHAPTER IV

AUSTRIA.

BY JOHANNA LEITENBERGER.

[Mrs. Johanna Leitenberger was born at Prague, Bohemia, in 1818. She published, at an early age, some lyric poems and prose essays which met with a favorable reception. After her marriage, separate volumes in prose and poetry began to appear, and an historical tragedy (*Veronika von Teschenitz*) was played with great success at the two theatres of Gratz. Mrs. Leitenberger edited the *Women's Journal* (*Frauenblätter*), devoted to the progress and instruction of women, which was published for a year and a half in this same city. In 1873 Mrs. Leitenberger traveled in Northern Italy and Southern France, and gave in several newspapers an account of what she saw. The next year she established herself at Salzburg, where she still resides, and where were written a collection of tales (*Lichtstralen*) and some religious poems (*Schneeglöckchen*). Mrs. Leitenberger is a contributor to many journals in both Austria and Germany.]

AUSTRIA-HUNGARY is composed of so many peoples of different language and origin, that, although they are all under one government, it is very difficult to give a precise account of this whole vast and varied agglomeration. Prince Gortchakoff's famous remark, that Austria is not a state but a government, is, perhaps, not wholly devoid of truth. But the other races of the Empire are grouped around the old German stock, which, in many respects, stands at the head of civilization and progress. This sketch, therefore, will have to do chiefly with the German women of Austria, for the women of the other parts of the Empire, and especially those of Hungary, have generally followed the lead of their German sisters in all movements for the amelioration of woman's condition. This preponderance of the Teutonic influence in our society is brought out still more strongly by the fact, that the position of the sex in state and family, and the conduct of the government in regard to our interests and rights, is, in all essential particulars, the same in the Austrian Empire as in the German Empire.*

The women's movement in Austria has had two phases: the economic and the educational. It is astonishing what opposition the latter question has called forth, especially among men. They have brought forward every argument the most careful research could produce, with which to combat the proposition to instruct women and to prepare them for callings monopolized by the other sex. Learned professors have not hesitated to assert the intellectual inferiority of women and to expatiate on the weight and quality of their brains. But, notwithstanding this resistance, great progress has been made in the industrial and professional education of women. Institutions for the preparation of women for active employments are continually appearing everywhere in Austria. In the front rank stands the Women's Industrial Society (*Frauen-Erwerb-Verein*), which was founded at Vienna in 1866, and which has grown every year in usefulness and importance. In 1874 the Society opened its school for the industrial training of women, and workshops, art studios, schools of design, etc., soon

---

* Mrs. Schepeler-Lette, of Berlin, writes me: " Austria, although politically separated from Germany, is so closely bound to her by the ties of a common ancestry, that the history of the development of the women's movement in the latter country would be incomplete, if the history of the same movement in the former country were neglected."—T. S.

followed. A class in lace-making is connected with the school, and the children of the poor lace-makers of the Erzgebirge, of Bohemia, are here taught gratuitously. But the aim of the Society is not simply to train the hand : it would also develop the intelligence of its pupils. It has, therefore, established a commercial school, formed classes in the French and English languages, and during the winter season courses of lectures on various artistic and scientific subjects are delivered under its auspices by competent professors and scholars. Far more than a thousand women have, during the past few years, enjoyed the privileges of this admirable institution, of which Mrs. Jeannette von Eitelberger is the president. Many of the other principal cities of the Empire possess similar societies.

The State participates in the good work and confers honors on the friends of the movement. In 1875, for example, the government founded at Salzburg a school of trades, which contains a department for women who wish to study certain of the arts applied to industry. Orders of merit have been bestowed on Mrs. Jeannette von Eitelberger, whom I have just mentioned; Mrs. Emilie Bach, who is at the head of the Vienna school of art embroidery; and Mrs. Johanna Bischiz, president of the united women's societies of Buda-Pesth.

If now we turn to the general education of women, we find that great progress has been made during the past ten years, especially in Austria. The public and private schools for girls are infinitely improved. The establish-ment of girls' lyceums (*Lyceen*), which aim at the higher and broader education of women and which cover almost the same ground as the boys' gymnasiums, was a great step in advance, although they are far from meeting all the demands of the new era. Gratz has an excellent lyceum, and the mayor's wife took an active part in its creation. The normal schools for the training of female teachers are of a superior order in many of the Austrian cities. But they have turned out so large a number of pupils during the past few years, that many young teachers, after long months of waiting, are finally compelled to seek employment in private families.

Hungary also offers many signs of progress. The country possesses some four hundred organizations whose aim is the improvement of women's condition. A teacher of South Hungary writes me: " Here, too, the women's movement is a movement in advance, especially in the department of industrial pursuits or employments. Presburg, for example, has a society to encourage the employment of women. Many young girls of good family prepare themselves for teachers, although there is an oversupply in this profession, on account of the large number of Catholic sisters, who have of late invaded our school-rooms. These ecclesiastic teachers have gained possession of the girls' schools and kindergartens in every city and important town of South Hungary. Many young women, however, study the Fröbel system in the institutions for the training of kindergarten teachers at Buda-Pesth, Klausenburg and other places. Females also find employment in the telegraphic and postal service and in other departments of government. It is here that we find the most marked progress in the amelioration of the condition of Hungarian women."

If we approach South Austria, we meet with a goodly number of institutions for girls, as for instance at Laybach, in Carniola, where females are not only employed in the telegraphic and postal service, but are furnished the instruction necessary to fill these posts.* Girls may obtain private instruction in the commercial school of this same city. At Triest is a normal school which has been recently converted into a girls' lyceum. Primary schools for girls are found at Görtz, Fiume, and other cities in the south. Institutions of a higher grade for the instruction of women do not exist either in the maritime countries or in Dalmatia.

The Society of Austrian Teachers and Governesses (*Verein der Lehrerinen und Erzieherinen in Oesterreich*), founded in 1870, takes care of the intellectual and material interests of its members. Its work may be classed under three heads: 1. Normal school and scientific instruction. 2. The spreading of rational ideas on female education. 3. The aiding of needy members. These objects are accomplished by lectures and discussions on pedagogic and scientific themes, by the use of a library and reading-room, by participation in teachers' meetings and congresses, by the publication of the proceedings of the society in the newspapers, by gratuitous information to those seeking situations, by the setting apart of a fund for the sick, etc., etc. The Society supports a Home, which can at present accommodate eleven persons, and offers to teachers and governesses, during their sojourn at Vienna, a good, healthy, cheap boarding-house. The Society organizes lotteries from time to time, the prizes being various kinds of women's work. The net proceeds of the lottery of 1881 were turned over to the Home. This admirable organization is

---

* A recent law has, unfortunately, prohibited the further employment of women in this field. Those already in the service may, however, remain. The reason given for this unjust change is that the male telegraphists complained that the females worked for too low wages!—J. L.

under the able management of Mrs. Louise von Stahl-Almásy.

There are many women's charitable societies at Vienna and in the other Austrian cities. Among those at the capital may be mentioned a society for the maintenance of the widows and orphans of musicians (the *Haydn*), which was founded some twelve years ago ; an asylum for homeless women (the *Elizabethinum*), under the protection of the Empress, which, in the single month of February, 1882, came to the aid of 1,496 women and 407 children ; an aid society whose aim is to instruct and train Jewish girls for some trade; an asylum (*Töchterheim*) for the orphan daughters of Government officials; a retreat for poor and friendless women and girls (*Frauenheim*), which was established in 1882; the Housekeepers' Society (*Hausfrauen-Verein*), which has an intelligence office and a shop for the sale of women's work; a society (*Gisela-Verein*) under the patronage of the Archduchess Gisela, eldest daughter of the Emperor, which gives a dowry to poor marriageable young girls; and a women's society for the training of domestics. The Vienna Women's Charitable Society (*Frauen-Woltätigkeits-Verein*) has brought about the creation of similar institutions in many other Austrian cities. The Rudolph Society (*Rudolf-Verein*) has established at Vienna a school for the training of female nurses, and in 1881 its students were admitted to the clinics of the celebrated surgeon, Professor Billroth.*

---

* The Baroness Kathinka von Rosen, a zealous friend of this school, published in the autumn of 1881 a " Guide for Nurses of the Sick " (*Leitfaden für Krankenpflegerinen*), which is rich in personal experiences in English hospitals and in the military hospitals during the recent troubles between Servia and Turkey, and Russia and Turkey.—J. L.

The statistical report for 1881 furnishes the following interesting information concerning the female population of Vienna, and may be taken as a fair sample of the condition of women throughout the empire generally:

Government employées	20
Teachers	2,790
Authors and editors	25
Actresses and musicians	739
Painters and sculptors	53
Employées of the Board of Health	5
Health officers	870
Innkeepers	133
Farmers	4
Miners	2
In industrial pursuits	4,855
In business	4,448
In banks	14
Messengers	116
Living on their incomes	9,460
Living on pensions, and the like	5,154
Heads of educational establishments	32
Heads of charitable institutions	19
In undefined callings	31,518
Clerks	2,378
Day laborers	49,376
Domestics	75,238

That is, 187,249 women, out of 373,156—the female population of Vienna—do something toward their own support.

Although the doors of our universities are closed to females, we possess many women who have pursued their studies abroad and who have acquired a reputation for their learning. Miss Rosa Welt, of Vienna, for example, is a graduate of Bern. During the summer semester of 1879, she attended the lectures on ophthalmy of Professor Mauthner, of Vienna, was admitted to the Rothschild hospital, directed by Dr. Oser, and was at one time mentioned as likely to become the assistant of Professor Pflüger, of Bern, on diseases of the eye. The wife of Dr. Kerschbaumer, who has an institute at Salzburg for the cure of diseases of the eye, studied medicine at Vienna, became her husband's assistant, and now aids him in all operations and sometimes performs them herself. The orientalist, Mrs. Camilla Ruzicka-Ostoic, who has spent six years at the Imperial Academy of Oriental Languages in Vienna, and has passed brilliant examinations in Turkish, Russian and Arabic, received from the Emperor a gold medal for her dictionary of Turkish-German transcriptions, and from the King of Bavaria the Ludwig's gold medal for art and science. In 1881 she established at Vienna a private school for instruction in the Oriental tongues and gave free courses of lectures to ladies on the Turkish language. Miss Sofie von Torma has done some very good work recently in the investigation of antiquities at Siebenbürgen. She has a book almost ready for publication in French and German, and has lectured on her discoveries. Professor A. H. Sayce, of Oxford, and Dr. Schliemann, have both spoken in high terms of Miss von Torma's excavations.* Miss Emilie Hörschelmann has lectured with success to women in Vienna on the history of art. Miss Amalie

---

* In a letter from Athens, which I received in October, 1882, Dr. Schliemann says : " In commenting on my Trojan antiquities in ' Ilios,' I have continually pointed out the great similarity which exists between many of them as compared to the antiquities found in Hungary, and in my mind there can hardly be a doubt that in a remote prehistoric time Hungary was peopled by a Thracian race, which, as it would appear by the signs brought to light by Miss von Torma, also extended over Siebenbürgen. A lady who excavates is a very rare thing, and such efforts as hers ought to be encouraged and applauded by every archæologist. I twice mentioned her important excavations on page 350 of my ' Ilios.' "—T. S.

Thilo, principal of an important girls' institute at the capital, is well known for her lectures on pedagogics, that on the great names in the history of education being specially worthy of mention. In 1881 Miss Helene Druskovich, Ph.D., spoke before a large audience under the auspices of a Viennese society, and showed a large acquaintance with the Italian and other foreign literatures. Miss Susanna Rubinstein, Ph.D., has made a name both at home and abroad by her lectures and philosophical works. These are a few names selected from a long list of women who have proved that intellectual power is independent of sex.*

---

* The number of women who have shown real talent in special studies is much larger than is generally supposed. Every country furnishes examples similar to those given in the text. The London *Times* (weekly edition, January, 19, 1883) in a review of the " Dictionary of Christian Biography," refers in these terms to the female contributors : " One, Miss Dunbar, of Duffus, has very appropriately been intrusted with the account of a few saintly women. The other, Mrs. Humphry Ward, has contributed a series of learned and interesting articles on a subject which few scholars would have been competent to treat. * * * It will be only necessary to refer to her article on Leovigild to see that she holds a distinguished place among the contributors, not only in respect of her command of the learning connected with her subject, but in point of independent judgment and literary ability. * *. * " Here is another example which I find in the *Journal des Débats*, September 26, 1880 : In the sitting of Friday, September 24, 1880, of the Academy of Inscriptions and Belles-Lettres, M. Le Blant presented to the learned body, in the name of the Countess Lovatelli, a notice on a marble crater found in 1875 in the vineyard of the old monastery of St. Anthony on the Esquiline. " The author describes and interprets the figures which ornament this monument," said M. Le Blant, " and shows that she is perfectly well acquainted with the monuments of art and with Greek literature, whose original texts are familiar to her." At the German Anthropological Congress, held at Berlin in 1880, two or three women took seats as members along side of such savants as Virchow and Schliemann. Miss J. Mestorf and Professor Virchow served together on one of the committees.—T. S.

I shall next take up the part which women play in the fine arts in Austria. The theatre, especially during the past few years, has become a veritable magnet for every girl who feels that she possesses a particle of dramatic talent. A large number of our actresses and singers are famous abroad as well as at home. I may mention, for example, Mrs. Amalie Friedrich Materna, the daughter of a humble schoolmaster of Styria, who is to-day one of the most renowned prima-donnas of Austria and Germany; Mrs. Marie Wilt, Mrs. Ehnn, Miss Bianchi, etc. From the Imperial Theatre of Vienna I select the names of Wolter, Hartman, Wessely and Hohenfels. Outside of the theatres, a large number of women devote themselves to vocal and instrumental music, a taste which is greatly encouraged by the many musical societies scattered all over the country. Women generally prefer the piano, but the harp, zithern, the violin and harmonium have their votaries. The number of female composers is as yet small. In painting our women have made great progress during the past few years, as is evidenced by the art exhibitions which have occurred in various parts of the country. There are very few female sculptors.

Many of our women devote themselves to scientific literature and belles-lettres. Besides those already mentioned, I may cite Aglaja von Enderes, who has written on natural history; Eufemia von Koudriaffsky, who died in 1881, and who has often treated scientific subjects in her essays; Mrs. Elise Last, who published a few years ago "More Light" (*Mehr Licht*), an admirable exposition of the teachings of Kant and Schopenhauer; and Mrs. Charlotte Edle von Schickh, who also writes on philosophical subjects. Educational questions occupy the attention of many female authors. Austria has a large number of poetesses. Betty Paoli, the *nom de plume* of Elisabeth Glück, is distinguished for the strength and beauty of her verse ; the poetry of Margarethe Halm (Berta Maytner) is full of originality ; and Ada Christen (Christine Frederick) has published poems, dramas and novels. In lyric and epic poetry are found the names of the Countess Wilhelmine von Wickenburg-Almásy, Marie von Najmájer, a Hungarian by birth ; Caroline Bruch-Sinn, the Baroness von Kapri, the Baroness Josefine von Knorr, Angelika von Hörman, Herma Czigler von Eny-Vecse, and Constanze Monter (Rosa Pontini). Among our novelists are the Baroness von Ebner Eschenbach, Therese von Hansgirg, Hermine Proschko, Mrs. von Weissenthurn, and Louise Lecher. Ida Pfeiffer is a well-known writer on travels. She twice circumnavigated the globe, visited the countries of the north, Jerusalem and the island of Madagascar, and described her voyages in a simple, clear, and interesting manner. She died in 1858. Rosa von Gerold has recently published a fascinating account of an autumnal journey in Spain. Several very able works on spiritualism are due to the pen of the Baroness Adelma von Vay, *née* Countess Wurmbrand. Hedwig von Radics-Kaltenbrunner and Harriet Grünewald have written sketches, essays, etc., for different periodicals. Many women have treated the various aspects of the woman question. The poets, Rosa Barach and Henriette Auegg, have written on this subject. The essays and poems of Margarethe Halm are pervaded by a bold reformatory spirit. The Hungarian author, Ida von Troll-Borostyáni, published a volume on this question a short time ago, and Franzeska von Kapff-Essenther has handled the same theme in a novel.*

---

* Heinrich Gross, professor of German literature in the German State

Several newspapers are devoted to the different phases of the women's movement in Austria. Some years ago an ex-officer, Captain A. D. Korn, who, if I am not mistaken, had passed some time in England and America, founded the *Universal Women's Journal (Allgemeine Frauen Zeitung)*. This newspaper was wholly devoted to women's interests, but it soon died. The same thing is true of the *Women's Journal (Frauenblätter)* of Gratz, which appeared for a short time under the editorship of the writer of this sketch. Mr. Karl Weiss (Karl Schrattenthal), who is professor of German literature in the State college at Deva, recently established at Vienna a paper bearing a similar title (*Frauenblätter*), which suspended publication after the third or fourth number.

On the 9th, 10th, and 11th of October, 1872, the third German Women's Convention (*Deutsche Frauenkonferenz*) was held at Vienna, under the auspices of the General Society for Popular Education and the Amelioration of Women's Condition (*Allgemeine Verein für Volkserziehung und Verbesserung des Frauenloses*). The other two meetings of this society had been held at Leipsic and Stuttgart. The soul of this new movement was Captain Korn, whom I have already mentioned. His study of the woman question in the United States may have prompted him to awaken a similar agitation among the women of the Austrian Empire.* Addresses were delivered at this convention by ladies from Vienna, Hungary, Bohemia and Styria, and

---

school at Triest, published in 1882 a work on German female poets and authors. He is now (1883) engaged on an anthology of the female poets of Germany.—J. L.

* Several years ago Captain Korn and his wife, who took an active part in this convention, returned to Hungary, his native land, and I have never heard of him since. I do not even know whether he is still living.—J. L.

all the various interests of women were discussed. The author of this sketch read two essays—one on women's work and wages, the other on the education of women. The convention decided to petition for certain reforms. A resolution was adopted, amidst general applause, that monuments ought to be erected at Vienna and Presburg to the memory of the great Empress, Maria Theresa. Another resolution called for the enactment of a law which should assure women the same pay as men for the same work. The proceedings of the convention attracted considerable attention, and produced a favorable impression on the audience, which was recruited from the better classes of the population. But the newspapers of Vienna ridiculed the young movement, its friends grew lukewarm, and every trace was soon lost of this first and last Austrian Women's Rights Convention.

The legal position of women in Austria does not differ essentially from what it is generally among Teutonic and Latin nations. They are subordinated to men. A woman of the nobility loses her title on marrying a commoner, and her children cannot inherit it. If a woman lives five years outside of her country without an official permit, she becomes a foreigner. The married woman who has the right to vote, must exercise the privilege through her husband, but the widow and single woman may delegate any man to represent them at the polls.*

To sum up the situation, we find that in the field of labor the most crying need is the prompt and better sale of women's handiwork. Although bazaars and lotteries have been constantly employed for the purpose, there still remains much to be done in this direction. Radical innovations are needed in the system of women's instruction. The gymnasiums and universities should be opened to them. But as a vast majority of men, public opinion and a large number of women themselves are opposed, or at least indifferent, to this question, much time, agitation and popular enlightenment will be necessary to bring about this very desirable reform. But the future is not all darkness. I. H. von Kirchmann, the distinguished author, in his recently published work entitled, " Questions and Dangers of the Hour" (*Zeitfragen und Abenteuer*), devotes a division of his volume to " Women in the Past and Future," where he shows that the female sex has been gradually gaining its freedom, and predicts that the day is approaching when women will obtain their complete independence and will compete with men in every department of life, not excepting politics. Among our educated women great interest is shown in this question, but the female sex in general has never thought on it. It is a great impediment to progress and reform that Austria is composed of so many separate races, speaking different languages and having dissimilar customs and aims. The German, Hungarian, Slavonic and Italian peoples, which make up the Empire, do not all think alike and do not all work in unison. Thus, lack of interest on the part of the great mass of our women, and want of national unity in the Empire, are immense obstacles to the triumph of our movement. But I feel convinced that the day will come, when these races will unite in their efforts to ameliorate woman's lot, however much the ways and means employed to attain this end may vary, according to the different qualities and characteristics of these nations.

CHAPTER V

RUSSIA

BY MARIE ZEBRIKOFF.

[Miss Marie Zebrikoff was born in 1835, at Cronstadt, her father being an officer in the navy. She received a home education, which was broadened by extensive reading, and she published in 1868 her first critical essay, a review of the female characters of Leo Tolstoi's "Our Grandmothers." Similar articles followed, and the works not only of Russian authors but of Spielhagen, Auerbach, Shelley, George Sand, George Eliot and the other English female novelists, were criticised by Miss Zebrikoff's keen intellect in the pages of such periodicals as the *Contemporary Annals* (*Otechestvennya Zapiski*), *Herald of Europe* (*Viestnik Evropy*), *The Word* (*Slovo*), *The Act* (*Dielo*), and *The Week* (*Nédiclia*). From 1875 to 1880 Miss Zebrikoff was at the head of an educational review, and at the same time edited, translated and compiled many English, French, and German books, as, for example, Mrs. Ellet's "Women of the American Revolution" (compiled with an historical essay as a preface); "The Three First Years of a Child's Life" (*Les Trois Premières Années de l'Enfant*), by Bernard Pérez, (translated); John Morley's "On Compromise" (translated with an essay); "The Emile of the Nineteenth Century," (*L'Emile du XIXᵉ Siècle*), by Alphonse Esquiros (translated), and "The New Life" (*Neues Leben*), by the late Berthold Auerbach. One of Michelet's histories, translated by some ladies, was edited and introduced to the public by Miss Zebrikoff in aid of the courses for the higher education of women—mentioned in the following pages—of whose exective committee she is a member. Miss Zebrikoff is a contributor to many educational periodicals, and is the author of some children's books.]

AN American woman—Miss Blackwell—was the first to open to her sex the untrodden path of medical science; a Russian woman, Miss Nadiejda Souslova, was the second.* Nearly twenty years have elapsed since that day, and Russian women have given many shining proofs of their ability, their perseverance and their courage, and have won academic distinctions in numerous universities of Europe. This remarkable innovation, in a field considered too rough for women's weak feet and forbidden them by popular prejudices, which, alas! are still too strong, has been a source of great astonishment alike to every friend and enemy of the woman question. I have often been asked, in my travels in Germany and Switzerland, the following question: "How is it that Russia, which by no means occupies the foremost rank in European civilization, is first in this matter of women's emancipation?—for no country in the Old World can vie with Russia in this respect." The answer to this question cannot be given in a line, but requires an explanation of some length.

Every new movement, however slight it may be, has its roots deep down in the national life. The great and successful impulse of Russian women toward scientific education is due to causes which spring from the political and social state of the country. Russia, although she came later than the other nations of Europe to work in the vineyard of modern civilization, has reaped certain benefits from this very tardiness. Hers is the lot of the youngest brother, who strives to emulate the best qualities of his seniors, but whose eyes are open to their defects,

---

* Miss Souslova, daughter of a peasant who had acquired some fortune, was the first Russian woman graduated in medicine at a foreign university, Zurich. Graduates of foreign medical schools, in order to practice in Russia, must submit to an examination in that country. Miss Souslova passed her Russian examinations so brilliantly that she astonished our medical celebrities, and has since won the reputation of being a very able physician. She has a very large practice in St. Petersburgh.—M. Z.

errors, and faults, and who grows wiser by their experience, seeking a lofty ideal which they have yet to attain. This lateness, therefore, has assigned to Russia a peculiarly important part in the work which the other nations are called upon to perform.

Although the historical antecedents of the United States and Russia are as widely separated as the poles, the former being freedom-seeking Europe removed from its old dwelling-place to a new one, still there are some striking points of likeness between the Russian Autocracy and the American Republic. The most remarkable of these resemblances is that both countries are thoroughly democratic. We may in some respects apply to Russia the following sentiments addressed by Goethe to the United States:

> Amerika Du hast es besser
> Als unser Continent das alte,
> Hast keine verfallenen Schlösser
> Und keine Basalte,
> Dich stört nicht im Innern
> Zu lebendiger Zeit
> Unnützes ·Erinnern
> Und vergeblicher Streit.*

We have had no feudal aristocracy which made women slaves and victims to the dynastic interests of the family, and which, though modified by the vivifying breath of the eighteenth century, is still a formidable stumbling-block to the advance of liberty and equality in Europe. In spite of the old barriers dividing the nobles from the merchant and peasant classes, Peter the Great himself could not

---

* America, thou art much happier than our old continent; thou hast no castles in ruins, no fortresses; no useless remembrances, no vain enmity will interrupt the inward working of thy life. (*Den Vereinigten Staaten in Sprüche in Reimen*).—T. S.

engraft primogeniture upon our institutions. The nobility clung to the democratic custom of dividing the property equally among all the sons, so that no hereditary aristocracy was called into life. Women were thereby benefited. When there are no male heirs—that is, no sons—the property is divided equally among the daughters, and the mother receives one-seventh of the real estate and one quarter of the personal property. The widow or orphan daughters do not run the risk of being driven from their father's house, as is the case in England when an estate goes to a male heir of a collateral branch.*

The question of woman's emancipation was first openly discussed by our newspapers and became a factor in Russian progress when the chains of the serfs were broken on February 19th, 1861. The spirit of liberty and equality is like rising water: it cannot mount in one portion of society without reaching the same level in every part. In England, to take another example, the women's movement sprang into life when the emancipation of the workman became a burning theme in the press. in public meetings and in parliament. But the woman question in Russia has not yet emerged from the ideal phase, and can boast of but very few practical victories,—scarcely more

---

* There are many other examples of the democratic spirit in Russia. Before the time of Peter the Great all government offices were held by men of noble blood. The aristocracy (*boyars*) and the gentry (*dvorianstvo*) divided among themselves the few positions which then existed in the crown service. Since Peter the Great, not birth but education has been the necessary qualification. The son of a peasant, merchant or mechanic, if he has been educated at an intermediate school (*gymnasium*), is a candidate for a place under government. Since the abolition of slavery, in the last reign, all Russians have been placed on the same level of equality. There is but one exception,—peasants, workmen, and small shopkeepers may be punished with the rod.—M. Z.

than three. Our women are mistresses of their own fortune; they participate in the choice of members of the municipal council and county assembly, through the agency of a male friend or relative who represents them at the polls, and they enjoy the means of securing a higher education, wrung by their own brave efforts from the reluctant hands of society and the bureaucracy. The first two privileges have come down to Russian women from the centuries, while in liberal England they have only recently been secured, and in republican France they are utterly unknown.*

Notwithstanding these advantages, the condition of the Russian woman as regards the relations between parents and children, and husband and wife, is that of a dependent being. As a daughter, she is in the absolute power of her parents until their death. On reaching her majority, she does not become free to act and think for herself. Her lot is complete obedience, except in the two cases where the parents incite their daughter to crime, or order her to do an illegal act. And even here, everything is against the daughter. She must prove the truth of her allegations before the courts—a very difficult proceeding where it is the vogue to surround all criminal actions with mystery, and witnesses are in bad odor.† The text of the Russian law is explicit. The authority of parents over their children ceases only with death, except in the case of a son entering the crown service or when a daughter

---

* Miss Zebrikoff might have added that the same thing is true of the United States as a whole, democratic and republican though they be.— T. S.

† Russian law considers women's testimony of less weight than that of men. A clause in the code reads : " When two witnesses do not agree, the testimony of an adult outweighs that of a child, and the testimony of a man, that of a woman."—M. Z.

marries, for, as the law reads, " one person cannot reasonably be expected to fully satisfy two such unlimited powers as that of the husband and that of the parents."* Obedience to parents, therefore, cannot be required of a married daughter to the same extent as of her unmarried sister.

Parents have the right to punish the rebellious child, and both the secular and ecclesiastical authorities are armed by the law with power to aid them. On a simple request made by the parents, without any judicial examination, the child may be sent to the house of correction, sentenced to hard labor, or confined in a monastery, there to undergo religious discipline in the form of vigils, fasts, and prayers, and to be subjected to hardships scarcely less severe than those of the house of correction. Happily Russian society has outgrown these barbarous laws, and instances of their application are extremely rare, and always occasion a great hue and cry. They are, however, sometimes enforced. Ten years ago the newspapers told of three men, one thirty-five, the other two seventeen and twenty years respectively, who were sent to the house of correction for four months, not as a punishment for the very grave crimes of which they were guilty—one of them had nearly committed murder in a fit of intoxication—but simply, on the demand of their parents, to restrain them from going to greater excesses. The youth of seventeen and the man of thirty-five were imprisoned at the instance of a widowed mother, a poor music teacher, struggling for her own and her daughter's sustenance, while the third owed his confinement to a widow of seventy, who trembled for the future of her youngest son.

---

* Volume X. of the Russian Civil Laws.—M. Z.

It will have been noticed that the Russian mother is on a footing of equality with the father in exacting filial obedience. The slave of yesterday may be a tyrant to-day, if a mother whose husband allows her some freedom of action, or if a widow. It will also have been observed that the same submission is required of the son as of the daughter, except when the former enters the service of the State. Neither may marry without the parents' consent. In but two provinces of Russia—Pultava and Chernigoff—a daughter, on attaining the age of twenty-one, may take legal measures to force her parents to consent, and then only when the father or mother is guardian of the property belonging to her.* Women, however, derive but little benefit from this law, as it is applicable only to those who possess property, and who have lost one of their parents, so that the surviving parent is the guardian of this property; or to those who, both parents living, have inherited property.

If the girl is not free in her choice of a husband, the parents cannot force her to take a husband against her will. If she may not marry the man of her choice, she can at least remain single. Peter the Great established this law prohibiting marriage where one of the contracting parties objected. The priest may not begin the ceremony if the bride declares that her parents have forced her to accept the groom. But it must be borne in mind that the assertion of this right requires no small amount of moral courage on the part of the young girl, who, after the

---

* Pultava and Chernigoff were a part of Little Russia, formerly an independent state of Zaporogue Cossacks, who, to escape from the thraldom of Poland, submitted to Russia on the condition that their laws and customs should be respected. This is the origin of the exception referred to in the text.—M. Z.

public scandal occasioned by such a declaration, must return to parents irritated at her disobedience, and, as their conduct proves, wanting in all true affection for her. But to-day such marriages never occur among the educated classes,—a proof of progress in civilization, and at the same time of independence among our young women.

The Russian marriage laws are a little less severe than those of Catholic origin. Civil marriage is unknown. Marriage is a religious rite—a sacrament—and is indissoluble except on three or four grounds. A great and salutary victory will be gained when the marriage laws of Russia are radically reformed. Ill-usage and immorality are not considered sufficient causes for divorce. By marriage, a woman becomes the subject of an autocratic lord. With the exception of her dowry—for she is the absolute mistress of her own fortune—the wife is in the full power of the husband. If her choice proves unhappy, she must bear her lot. Her husband may be a dissolute drunkard, immoral, dishonest; but she remains his wife. If he ill-treats her, she may have him cast into prison by complaining to the justice of the peace, but she is still his wife when the term of punishment has expired. The law does not here recognize any ground for divorce.

There are but four cases in which divorce is granted in Russia. The first is physical incapacity for marriage either on the part of the wife or the husband, and in the latter case the wife must prove her virginity after three years of married life. The second is adultery by the husband, which must be established by two witnesses present at the moment the crime was committed, a requirement which renders proof of infidelity almost impossible. The third is the disappearance of the husband for a period of five years. In this case the wife may apply to an ecclesiastical council for the annulment of the marriage. But this court is as dilatory as it is venal. The divorce is granted only when the husband fails to answer the summons of the court, and the slightest rumor that he has been seen or heard of in some quarter, often protracts the proceedings to such an interminable length, that the poor wife loses both the bloom and strength of youth. The fourth and last ground for divorce occurs when the husband is deprived of his civil rights and is exiled to Siberia. The wife may follow her husband, but all children born after the father's disgrace are considered to belong to the lowest class in society, though the wife and the children born before his condemnation preserve their social position.* When the wife, taking advantage of her husband's degradation, applies for a divorce, the religious authorities grant the request, and the secular power gives her a pass,†

---

* Russian society is sharply divided into four classes, rising one above the other. The last and lowest is made up of peasants and the petty shopkeepers of the towns. They are looked down upon by all the other classes, and are subjected to corporal punishment for delicts. The wife who accompanies her husband to Siberia may see him and her children subjected before her own eyes to the degrading penalty of the rod.—M. Z.

† A *pass* is an official paper giving the name, rank, profession, etc., of the holder of it. Every Russian subject must have a pass. On arriving in any town, in changing lodgings and the like, the pass must be sent to the police to be viséed. When a woman marries, she is inscribed on her husband's pass, and if she wishes to visit another town, she must obtain a pass from him. Otherwise she may not leave him. This document is generally worded as follows: "I give this pass to my wife that she may inhabit any city or village she chooses." It depends entirely upon the husband to name the term for which the pass is good, and when it expires, the wife must return or get it renewed. The daughter stands in the same relation to her parents as the wife to the husband. They give her a pass, which is registered by the police and stamped. Among the working classes, the wife and daughter often obtain their pass only after paying a stipulated sum to the husband or parents.—M. Z.

stating her new condition. She may then re-marry. To the honor of Russian wives be it said, that few seek for a divorce under this fourth head, but rather, on the contrary, many share the lot of their exiled husbands, or remain behind only in order that their children may receive an education which could not be found in some remote Siberian village. The *via dolorosa*—the highway to Siberia—has often witnessed men staggering on under the weight of heavy chains, while their wives, with infants at the breast, follow on foot or in rough open carts.*

The Russian civil law recognizes a separation between husband and wife, but this must not be confounded with divorce. It occurs only when both parties consent to it, and neither has the right to marry again. The law gives the daughter to the father and the son to the mother, on the ground that the stronger should support the weaker. When the wife is without fortune, the husband is obliged to furnish the means for her maintenance and for the maintenance and education of the children, if there be any. If the wife willfully leaves her husband, he may force her to return to him, and if necessary call upon the police for aid. If a man of cruel nature, he may compel her to submit to an escort of armed policemen along with the vagabonds and criminals who are being conveyed from one prison to another. The late Third Section, or department of secret police, which has left behind it throughout all Russia such a loathsome and dreaded name,

---

* It is worthy of note that in this fourth case the church departs from its principle of the indissolubility of marriage, binding the wife to her husband for weal and for woe, and accepts the considerations of the civil law. It may be added that a marriage is null when unlawfully contracted, when the bride's protest was disregarded, when the man was married under a false name, etc.—M. Z.

had at least one redeeming feature, in that it frequently shielded women from brutal husbands. Often has its occult power snatched from the tyrant his victim whom the ecclesiastic and secular laws did not protect, and forced him to give her a pass which allowed her to live unmolested. If, on the other hand, the husband deserts his wife, she may claim from him enough money to support herself and children.

The pecuniary independence of the Russian woman—for she is mistress of her own fortune, as I have already stated—has led to her obtaining the few other privileges which she enjoys. As she owns property, she pays taxes, and therefore participates in the choice of the members of the municipal council *(gorodskaya ouprava)* which expends her money.* Women do not go to the polls themselves, as I have said before, but are represented by some male relative or friend who votes for them.† They choose in the same way the members of the county assembly, *(zemstvo)*, who appoint the board or committee which supervises the public affairs of the county.

These rights possessed by Russian women must not be measured by a European or American political standard. The powers of the municipal and county assemblies may

---

* The advocates of women's rights in the United States have been proclaiming for forty years that "taxation without representation is tyranny," while Russia, the land of autocracy, has been practicing this fundamental principle of justice since the days when we were colonies. Here, as in many other places in this book, Americans will notice that in our treatment of women we are often far behind what we are pleased to call "effete monarchies." —T. S.

† Mrs. Worden, Seward's sister-in-law, adopted a somewhat similar plan. She required all the men who worked on her farm near Auburn to vote as she wished, for, being a taxpayer and yet a widow without father or son, she felt that she ought to be represented at the polls.—"History of Woman Suffrage," I., 462.—T. S.

be likened to those of a housekeeper or an intendant of a great estate; they gather the taxes and expend them on schools, hospitals, roads and canals. But they may make no laws, vote no supplies, in a word, do nothing to change the ordained order of things. Yet the *gorodskaya ouprava* and the *zemstvo*, although they have no voice in legislating for the nation, nor even for their own province, county, or town, exercise a great influence in their narrow circle, and are a step toward self-government. Before their creation, the work which they now perform was in the hands of a crowd of government agents *(tchinovniks)*, who were an absolute plague to the country.

American women ask for participation in the enactment of the laws which they are bound to obey. But Russian women cannot make such a lofty demand, for men even do not enjoy this right. We can feel, however, that politically we are almost the equal of men, although we may not, like them, deposit our own votes and are not eligible to either of the public bodies of which we are electors.*

The Russian peasant women are in a much worse state than the women of the upper classes. They must obey not only the laws of the empire, but those of custom— a sort of common law—which vary in different provinces. Their lot is hard and miserable in the extreme, and our renowned poet, Nekrassoff, has given a vivid and pathetic picture of it in his poems. In Great Russia, that is, in all the provinces of north, east, and middle Russia, where the system of the village " commune " exists, these laws of custom protect women in some respects.

---

* Universal suffrage does not exist in Russia. The ownership of property or the payment of a certain tax is the necessary qualification of an elector. Every woman who meets this requirement, votes.—M. Z.

In these village communes, the land is considered to belong to all the inhabitants in common. The village council (*mir*), after the lapse of a certain period of years, divides the fields and meadows into lots, according to the number of families and the size of each family. A numerous household receives a larger lot than a small one. The father may not sell or mortgage his lot, but it is his for tillage until the new period of division comes round. If he concludes to abandon his peasant state and become a merchant or denizen of a town, his land reverts to the commune, though his cottage, cattle, furniture, harvest, carts, implements, etc., are considered to be his. The principle in the communes of Great Russia is this: the land belongs to the tiller of the soil, but only so long as he tills it.

This idea, firmly planted in the mind of the people, sometimes redounds to the advantage of the peasant women. When an industrious wife is tied to a worthless husband who is undermining the prosperity of the family, she complains to the *mir*, which often transfers the lot of land to the wife, who thus becomes, *de facto*, the head of the family. When a widow can, by her own and her children's exertions or by the aid of a hired man, cultivate her late husband's lot, she becomes its owner and has a voice in the *mir*. There are numerous examples of women continuing to represent the family, even after the eldest son has reached his majority. When a member of the commune enters the army, his wife is provided with a lot of land, if she is ready to cultivate it. An orphan girl, if she declares her intention not to wed, demands a similar favor. Girls generally marry in another than their own commune and rarely bring a husband into it, for otherwise, in either case, the new family would have to be given a lot, which would lessen the extent of the existing holdings.

This *mir* is a powerful and important little body. It often acts as a judge in quarrels between husband and wife; sees that the land is well cultivated; that the taxes are paid; and it names the school boards and the school patrons and patronesses.* I recall a curious instance of one of these patronesses, who, the daughter of a rich peasant, could neither read nor write, and who, with tears in her eyes, related how her father had forbade her acquiring these elementary branches of knowledge. But once appointed patroness by the *mir*, the father could no longer check her, and she finally learned to read and write by daily intercourse with the scholars in the school-room. The Russian *mir*, however, must not be thought, from these few instances of liberality, a friend of women's emancipation. It is only too ready to lend a helping hand to parents or husbands when they desire to crush the spirit of independence in daughter or wife.

Some communes unite, form what is called a *voloste*, and choose judges, who are appealed to in the case of small delinquencies, family differences, petty thefts, etc. I know of instances where this peasant justice has been favorable to women; as, for example, where a wife, declaring that she would drown herself rather than return to her husband, this *volostnoy* tribunal obliged the latter to give her a pass, so that she might earn her own livelihood as a domestic. Such decisions, although perfectly binding in the eyes of the peasants, are in reality illegal,

---

* There are three sorts of elementary schools as regards their origin: those founded by the government, by the *zemstvo*, and by private individuals. When the peasants create one of the third class, they choose a patron or patroness who has leisure and money to devote to the school.—M. Z.

148

as they are in opposition to the written code of the empire. No regularly-constituted court of justice could compel a husband to give his wife a pass, unless he chose to do so of his own free will.

Among the peasants, the bride's preferences are seldom heeded by the parents when they arrange her marriage, and it is but poor consolation that the bridegroom is treated in the same way. She must accept her fate, and bear it patiently unto death. In the words of Pope, slightly changed,

> She is but born to try
> The lot of man,—to suffer and to die.

She cannot take advantage of the divorce law in the few cases already mentioned, for the legal, medical, and other expenses are too large for a peasant woman's purse. Divorce is available to her only when her husband loses his civil rights.

The subject condition of Russian women is one of the principal causes of the rapid growth among the people of certain radical Christian sects, some of which resemble in many particulars the American revivalists and Anabaptists. The despotism of the family drives the peasant woman to these sects, which teach that there can be no domestic ties *de jure* where none exist *de facto*, and that it is degrading to observe the letter when the spirit is dead. She flies from her home, and lives under an assumed name, lest she be dragged back to her former servitude. She feels raised to a condition of equality and independence by her faith in a religious doctrine, and ardently embraces the new belief. The maiden, or woman married against her will by the State church, having once thrown in her lot with these enthusiasts,

149

may marry among them. Until within the last two years Russian law did not recognize these marriages, and *de jure* the wife was always free to leave her sectarian husband, without his being able to restrain her. In some of these sects, the husband and wife stand on an equal footing, and the marriage lasts as long as both parties are satisfied. On entering the conjugal state, they declare their intention before the elders of the church, and on sundering the union, they do the same. Until very recently these sects were persecuted, and many a peasant woman, by her devotion and heroism, has shown herself worthy of the martyr's halo. Women often preach, and the greater number of these religious bodies are distinguished for a high moral level, purity and tenderness of domestic life, which is all the more remarkable, when it is remembered that an entire dissolution of all family ties is permitted by some of their peculiar doctrines.

Besides the sects just mentioned, there are others of an ascetic nature, in which the women take vows of chastity and consecrate their lives to nursing the sick and studying the Bible. A new sect has very recently sprung up, whose distinguishing feature is the exaltation of woman. She is placed above man because she can give birth to another immortal being. Her pain and travail are so great, that exempting her from all other physical suffering and annoyance would be but a poor reward; she is entitled to the deepest gratitude and reverence of mankind.*

---

* It is not the Russian sectaries alone who award women a higher place than that generally given them. In 1506, C. Agrippa wrote a treatise entitled, "On the excellence of woman above that of man." (Legouvé, *père, Mérite des femmes*, p. xlii.) Toussenel, says M. Pelletan, "has appealed to physiology to prove the superiority of woman to man." (*La mère*, p. 362.) M. Valentin de Gorloff, the young French African traveller, has said: "The

Certain writers who have studied these religious phenomena, speak with great admiration of some young girls gifted with remarkable oratorical talents and wonderful depths of mystical thought. The sects to which they belong seek sanctity in the acts of every-day life. A member of one of them—a psalm-reading old maid—said to a proud bishop riding in a carriage: "Christ went barefooted."

The spirit of the Russian sectaries in favor of the emancipation of women shows what a vital hold the woman question has on even the lowest orders of our national life. What the upper and educated classes of women seek in the sciences, higher education, and the liberal professions, the poor, ignorant peasant women find in mystical religion.

The subject of women's emancipation was first called into life among the enlightened classes of Russia, about the year 1840, by the writings of George Sand. The new ideas were confined to a narrow circle of thinkers and authors, and continued in a latent form until the freedom of the serfs caused them to burst forth with renewed force. No agitation can be pure gold: there must be some alloy in it. Errors were mingled with the young movement, and enmity and calumny magnified the demand for freedom into a cry for the destruction of the family. We have grown wiser by the faults committed at the inception of the struggle, and to-day our claims can be considered subversive only by those who wish

men of the Touareg tribe are not allowed to have more than one wife, and she possesses the greatest influence, not only in domestic but in political affairs. The Touareg women are far more highly educated than the men. They can read and write well, they possess some musical talent, and their poems are celebrated in the desert." (London *Times*, weekly edition, April 28, 1882.)—T. S.

women to be ignorant and spiritless slaves. The Russian woman seeks knowledge and the professions, not for the purpose of destroying the family, but that she may serve it the better. She does not ask emancipation from duty, but emancipation from chains. The freedom she yearns for is not the freedom of giving loose rein to all the whims of unprincipled fancy. She wishes to have the liberty of marrying whom she will, of breaking the bond which binds her to an immoral husband, of enjoying every facility for earning her own livelihood, and of removing all obstacles thrown in the way of acquiring knowledge which may open to her the highest positions in life. She desires to be no longer a zero in public affairs, but an active working force.

The reforms of the last reign gave a great impetus to the movement for women's independence, though this was not one of the results intended. The bureaucratic reform caused the discharge from the public service of hundreds and thousands of office-holders and governmental agents; and their daughters, who up to this time had lived in a state of more or less ease, were now thrown suddenly out upon the world to support themselves. The liberation of the serfs had the same effect. Before this reform was accomplished, a vast number of small land-owners found they could make more money by teaching their slaves trades than by cultivating their fields. So they increased their slaves, instructed them in all kinds of mechanical work, hired them out in the towns, and required of them an annual payment of from twenty to thirty rubles,* and in the case of a skillful hand even a larger sum. When emancipation came, the masters re-

---

* A ruble is worth from seventy-five to eighty-six cents, depending on the coinage.—T. S.

ceived an indemnity for the lots of land given by them to the slaves employed in agriculture, but no compensation was made them for the artisan slaves who gained their liberty at the same time. The landlords were entirely unprepared for this revolution, and were forced to hire laborers and buy machines to do the work which formerly cost them nothing. Many of them were ruined, and their daughters had to shift for their own livelihood. Thus, hard necessity made welcome the notion of women's independence, which without these two influences would have long remained in the realms of theory, for no idea ever triumphs in actual life without the way being prepared for it by economic causes.

But it is in the field of education that the greatest progress has been made. The difficulties that this movement has encountered and at last overcome would require too much space for enumeration, and could be understood in their full significance only by Russians, or by those foreigners who are well acquainted with the country. They show the importance of the victory, and are a happy omen for the future.

The vastness of the Russian Empire and the paucity of its population are in one respect favorable to this movement. Russia is sadly lacking in intellectual workers. The numerous villages disseminated throughout her wide plains want teachers and physicians. The professional emancipation of women is not therefore threatened by that inveterate opposition observed in densely peopled countries which annually disgorge into America their surplus of population. Our *zemstvo* needs and pays for the education of physicians in the woman's medical school at St. Petersburg, and for teachers in the various normal schools of the country, on the condition that the women who enjoy these scholarships serve five years the county which grants them. This scarcity of brain force constrains even the government to further the cause of women. We had a striking example of this in the recent struggle with Turkey, when the war department was only too glad to avail itself of the assistance of female physicians for the army.

The moral and intellectual power of women is recognized not only by the progressive, but also by the retrogressive, element of Russian society, and the latter class does not hesitate to use it. When, in 1867, three ladies, delegated by some of their own sex, requested the late Minister of Public Instruction, Count Tolstoi, to establish university lectures for women, they were met by a decided refusal. Thereupon the professors of the St. Petersburg faculty, taking advantage of their right to lecture in public, opened, under the auspices of a committee of ladies who managed the enterprise, a course of lectures, which, while not so considered officially, were in fact instituted for women. Although these lectures were attended by both sexes, women alone were allowed to use the library and cabinets in connection with them, to be examined if they wished, and to receive certificates from the professors. Ten years had not elapsed when the same minister who, in 1867, forced the scheme for the higher education of women to begin life under the guise of public evening lectures, acquiesced in the plan of instituting at St. Petersburg superior courses for women. Count Tolstoi wished to introduce into Russia his classical system—a profound study of the Greek and Latin, in imitation of the German gymnasiums—but not having the necessary number of teachers, on account of the aversion of the youth to pursue the classics to the extent he desired, the minister hoped to render the idea popular by having these languages taught in the girls' schools. So women were invited to acquire Latin and Greek, in order to fill the new positions; and thus was Count Tolstoi glad to avail himself of women's learning, and thus was he brought over from an enemy to a very reluctant friend of women's higher education.

The honor of the initiative step in this movement belongs to Mrs. Konradi. In 1866 she addressed a letter to the members of the association of natural and physical sciences, which met that year in St. Petersburg, requesting them to do something for women's university education. Her letter met with warm sympathy, and from that moment our men of science* have taken an active part in the work, so that to-day Russian women may pursue their studies not only at the capital, but also at Moscow, Kief, Kasan, and, in a word, in almost all the provincial cities where universities exist.

The curriculum of studies at St. Petersburg is very extensive, and is divided into two grand divisions,—the historical and literary, and that of the natural sciences and mathematics. The latter embraces anatomy, physiology, botany, zoölogy, chemistry, physics, geology, mineralogy,

---

* The chemist Louguinin subscribes annually five hundred rubles to the St. Petersburg courses for women, and Professor Bestoujeff is always ready to assist needy girls who cannot pay the tuition fee of fifty rubles a year. The celebrated professor of physiology, Siechenoff, has lectured in aid of a fund for a physiological cabinet for women, while Professor Miller, Professor Ovsiannikoff, and others have contributed money. Mr. Mendeleieff, professor of chemistry, and Mr. Vagner, professor of zoölogy, have lectured in our courses without pay. All the other professors offer their services at the modest charge of two hundred and fifty rubles a year for one hour, five hundred rubles for two hours, and so on. The same spirit is shown in the other university centres! In Moscow the literary and historical courses are superintended by Professor Guerié, who founded them.—M. Z.

astronomy, cosmology, and mathematics even in the highest branches. Lectures on agricultural chemistry are delivered to those women who are preparing themselves for agricultural pursuits, and a series of lectures on the civil law is given annually. The same studies with modifications are pursued in the other towns.

The courses for women in St. Petersburg were opened in 1878. The students are divided into four classes, each class representing a year's work. An examination occurs annually for all the classes. The first examination for graduation took place in the summer of 1882, when ninety-nine young women secured degrees in the literary and historical department, and sixty-four in the scientific department. About nine hundred students attend these lectures every year, and up to September, 1882, two hundred and one new matriculations had been registered for the session of 1882-3.* These numbers are all the more remarkable when it is remembered that as yet women derive no practical advantage from these long years of study, for, while the aim of the courses is to fit graduates for positions in the higher classes of girls' schools, men alone may fill them. Every man who desires a place in the intermediate schools must pass a teacher's examina-

---

* These figures prove that women desire a university education as much as men. This fact is almost universally accepted in the United States, though, as a general rule, it is only just beginning to dawn on the continental mind. Few American universities can boast of as many students and annual graduates as this St. Petersburg institution. The curriculum of studies destroys another objection to women's higher education almost as prevalent in the new world as the old, viz., that women are not capable of pursuing the same studies as men. If now the St. Petersburg reformers could only bring about co-education—a very easy step it would seem under the circumstances—they would be on the high road to the ideal educational system of the future.—T. S.

tion before the university authorities. Now our courses prepare women for these very examinations, from which, however, they are excluded. The professors of the University of St. Petersburg, and the members of the committee superintending the women's courses, have petitioned the government to admit women to the teachers' examinations. No answer has yet been given, but when it comes, it will doubtless be a favorable one, for a refusal would leave unsatisfied one of the most crying wants of Russian education.

The intermediate girls' schools (gymnasiums, as they are called), though they are far from perfect, are evidently considered a *pia desideria* in France, for a short time ago the French government sent a commission to Russia to study them. They owe their origin to the late Empress Maria Alexandrovna, who modeled them after the German *Töchter Schulen*. The course of studies covers seven years, and embraces the Russian, French, and German languages; arithmetic, and the rudiments of the sciences; but falls far short of what is needed for entrance into the university. This gap has to be filled by private study, and herein lies the grave defect of these schools.

The Minister of Public Instruction has established girls gymnasiums which lengthen the course of studies to eight years. These schools, although a thorough reform of the scope of their instruction is needed, have done a great and good work in spreading knowledge through the middle classes of Russian society, without, however, bridging the break just mentioned.

Government institutes, founded by the Empress Catherine II., and patterned after Madame de Maintenon's Maison de Saint-Cyr, of the time of Louis XIV., were the only girls' intermediate schools which existed in

Russia previous to the gymnasiums. Unlike the latter, class distinctions are observed in these institutes. Some of them receive the daughters only of the hereditary nobility, or of military and civil officers of high rank, while in others are educated girls from the families of the lesser nobility, of rich merchants, and of clergymen. The pupils are shut up in these schools from the age of seven or eight, until they reach their sixteenth, seventeenth, or even eighteenth year, and during this long period they seldom leave them, except on great holidays, and at the summer vacation. The instruction is superficial, and the scholars go forth entirely unprepared for real life. The gymnasiums are much preferable, as they do not separate the girl from her family, and from the active, practical world without.

Considered from a pedagogic standpoint, the gymnasium can fit its pupils only for the primary schools or for the lower classes of the gymnasiums. The government, in order to complete this deficiency, established, some time ago, a series of courses on pedagogics, which cover three years, and prepare teachers for the middle classes of the gymnasiums. This action was taken after the presentation of the petition asking for the admission of women to the teachers' examinations, which thus seems to have had some effect on the authorities.

The highest professional instruction for women is given in the medical courses, which began in a way that may appear strange to those not acquainted with Russian life. A young woman gave fifty thousand rubles for this object, but the sum was not large enough to cover all the expenses of the proposed school, and the undertaking would have fallen through if the War Department had not come to its aid. The Minister of War patronizing the medical education of women seems odd at the first blush. But his conduct was in fact very natural and very practical. The Academy of Medicine was already under the superintendence of the Minister of War, its chief aim being the education of surgeons for the army and navy, and, as it occupied a very large building, a part was handed over to the women for lecture rooms and clinics.*

The tentative of the government was very timid, not to say amusing. The female graduates were to be called "learned midwives;" † they were to study only the diseases of women and children; and when they went forth to practice the healing art, women and children were alone to be their patients. But the Minister of War builded better than he knew. The professors were real men of science, and found it impossible to keep within the narrow limits prescribed by the government. They gave a full course in medicine, added a fourth year, and then a fifth year, threw open the wards of the hospitals to their new pupils, and, in a word, treated the women just as they treated the men. And Russia was soon a thousand-fold

---

*Since these lines were written the medical instruction of women at the capital has entered upon a severe crisis. Recent reforms in the War Department call for economy, and the Minister has been forced to refuse the usual subsidy and to close the hospital and clinics. The St. Petersburg municipality offers to take the women under its protection, and furnish them a building and a hospital. Nothing is yet decided in the matter. The women who are now (October, 1883) studying will be allowed to finish their course, but no new students will be received. A public subscription, in aid of the Women's Medical Courses, has been opened at the capital. A women's medical college is about to be founded at Moscow, but it will, unfortunately, be far less complete than the St. Petersburg courses. —M. Z.

† This was the term used in the government plan, and was meant to distinguish the women who had received a scientific medical education from ordinary midwives.—M. Z.

repaid for what it had done. Twenty women followed the army in the last war, and gave admirable proofs of courage, skill, and tenderness on many battle-fields and in the hospitals, amid the ravage of the typhoid fever. The late emperor, who witnessed their conduct, always entertained a high opinion of them.

There are now in St. Petersburg fifty-two female physicians, and about two hundred and fifty in all Russia, although it is not yet ten years since medicine was opened to women. Many Russian women have also pursued their medical studies abroad in the Universities of Zurich, Bern, and Paris. I may also mention as among the professional institutions frequented by women, a school for the training of nurses, and two schools of midwifery in St. Petersburg, and one in Moscow. Women also study obstetrics in many of the hospitals.

I shall say nothing of the School of Painting at St. Petersburg, which owes its foundation to an association of artists and friends of art, and which receives students of both sexes; nothing of the Industrial Gymnasium, where girls are taught various trades, and which is a creation of the government; nothing of the good work done by the Froebel Society of St. Petersburg; nothing of the association formed two years ago at the capital for the establishment of girls' industrial schools, and to which one lady contributed 20,000 rubles,—but shall hasten on to the more important subject of the employment of women.

The elementary public schools offer our women the largest field of work. But the pay is so poor that men generally seek other callings, though there are many persons of both sexes who devote their lives to this humble occupation. The rôle is a difficult one and requires great fortitude and self-sacrifice, and yet many young girls take it up with genuine ardor. In some remote parts of Russia the schoolmistress is cut off during the long winter months from all intercourse with the world. She toils many hours each day for a beggarly reward; sees no books, reviews nor newspapers; lives in a log cabin deprived of all comforts; eats coarse food, and very seldom enjoys the society of persons of equal culture. And yet, notwithstanding all this devotion and acknowledged ability, the teacher's profession is, in the case of women, stunted in a most lamentable manner. They may instruct in elementary schools and in the lower classes of girls' gymnasiums and institutes, they may be governesses in private families, but they may aspire to nothing higher.

In medicine, we find similar restrictions. Although they pursue all the studies and pass all the examinations, women are not physicians in the eyes of the law. They may treat the diseases of women and children, but that is all. In the country, where there is often no male physician within the distance of fifty miles, our women might have employment and confer immense blessings upon the poor peasants of both sexes. Some years ago a woman passed a brilliant examination and defended with success a thesis on the diseases of the eye. But she could not become an oculist. And yet women, by the delicacy and flexibility of their fingers, are far better fitted physically than men for this calling. There have been instances of some of the medical inspectors in the provinces interfering with the practice of medicine by women, although invited by the *zemstvo* to come into their midst, by prohibiting the apothecaries to put up a prescription emanating from a female physician.

Some time ago an attempt was made to open the

law to women. After the reforms in our judiciary and the establishment of the order of advocates, some law offices employed women. Professors were invited to lecture on law before the women's courses at St. Petersburg, and some women went abroad to study the science in foreign universities. But the government forbade lawyers to accept their services as clerks, and the movement was nipped in the bud.

The government employs women only in the Fourth Section, the Department of the Empress, which directs the girls' gymnasiums and institutes. Women also find something to do in the railroad and telegraphic service. In the latter department they perform the hardest work, receiving and sending telegrams, while the much easier and better paid positions, as chief clerks and the like, are closed against them. Female telegraphists are paid only from twenty-five to forty rubles a month.

Women have yet to fight their way into the republic of the sciences. No woman has ever received a degree in our universities, while those who have been more successful abroad—and the list is long and brilliant—have asked in vain to be permitted to pass the examinations and defend the thesis for the degree of master of sciences. No positive law exists which bars women from securing university honors, for such a case was never foreseen. This fact is considered to be favorable to the claims of female aspirants. Mrs. Kovalevsky* and Mrs. Litvinova, doctors of mathematics of foreign universities, are now preparing themselves for the degree of master of sciences. If this stronghold is once gained, women will have the right to become professors in the superior courses for women.

---

* Mrs Kovalevsky has just (October, 1883) been appointed *privat-docent* at a college in Stockholm, and will lecture on mathematics.—M. Z.

There are many fitted for this career by their talents and learning who cannot enter upon it for lack of these degrees.

The scientific societies are more liberal than the universities. They do not shut their doors in our faces. The law society of St. Petersburg counts among its members Miss Evreinova, who took her degree of doctor of laws at Paris. The medical society is not afraid to affiliate with female physicians. Miss Nadiejda Skvortzova, whose ability has been recognized by the Paris medical celebrity, Dr. Charcot, is one of the women more recently received by this society.

It is in literature alone that women stand on the same footing with men.* This success depends entirely upon their talents. No certificate or degree here obstructs their path. But if a woman would enter journalism, if she would be the editor of a political or scientific newspaper, the case is different. When Mrs. Konradi, whom I have already mentioned in connection with women's higher education, and who is well known by her writings, wished to edit *The Week* (*Nediclia*), a political journal, permission was refused her by the censor of the press, and she had to put her husband forward as the nominal editor, though he was in no respect qualified for the position. Women may be editors of educational reviews, children's papers, eclectic magazines, and the like, and they may

---

* They are paid the same as men. The best known female writers receive as high as two hundred rubles for sixteen printed magazine pages, containing from 30,000 to 40,000 letters. The average remuneration is fifty, sixty, or seventy rubles, depending upon the reputation of the author and the popularity of the magazine. Many women support themselves by translating, but, as Russians are generally proficient in foreign languages, the market is overstocked and the pay is fifteen rubles or less for sixteen printed pages. The price for scientific translations is twenty-five rubles.—M. Z.

act as publishers of newspapers, reviews and books without having to make application to the censor. There are at St. Petersburg four or five children's papers and educational reviews which are edited by women, and one or two literary and political periodicals which are published by them.

The novel is the branch of literature in which Russian women have gained the highest reputation. After the two renowned names of Tourguéneff and Leo Tolstoi, the greatest novelist of which our literature can boast is a woman, Krestovsky,* the pseudonym of, Mrs. Nadiejda Zayontchkovsky. During a long literary career, which extends over a period of about thirty years, she has given to the world a large number of tales and novels of first-rate merit, and presents the rare example of a genius which, instead of weakening by the advance of age, grows in strength and depth. I know of no woman in European literature who is her equal, an opinion which is generally accepted. She may be compared to George Eliot. Inferior to the Englishwoman in the profundity of philosophical thought, she surpasses her in the warmth and vividness of her pictures. Her short stories are much better than the long ones, and all aim to depict some phase of Russian society. They are pervaded by the spirit of one seeking a lofty ideal, of a great-hearted patriot bleeding for the woes of her country, a lover of all that is pure and humane, a hater of all that is base and tyrannical. Many of Krestovsky's best pages have not been made public for political reasons. The freedom

---

* Krestovsky (pseudonym) is, as I have said in the text, an authoress. There is also a man, whose real name is Krestovsky, who writes sensational novels in which he paints in very dark colors the young generation striving for liberty and women seeking their emancipation. There is not much danger, however, of the two writers being confounded.—M. Z.

with which she lays bare the faults of our society may appear to be poor patriotism to those who take a narrow view of this feeling, and who too often magnify their own personal vanity into a national sentiment. There is a Russian proverb which reads : Who loves well, chastens well. But the dire necessity of chastening is a source of deep moral suffering.

This feature of Russian character, as reflected in our literature, is generally misunderstood, and yet it is one of the surest signs of our progress. It is a proof that the conscience of the nation is not lulled to sleep by self-adoration, but wide awake to the duty of striving to attain the loftiest ideal of human perfection. Russian society does not present the same comparative uniformity of level which, in spite of all the differences of parties, opinions and classes, exists in Europe and America. With us, one may see side by side representatives of the ideas of a hundred years ago, of the present century and of the ages to come, when the opinions which now count but few adherents will receive the right of citizenship in the world. Russian progress may be compared to an army's painful march through deserts and swamps, where the vanguard is so far in advance of the main body that it is supported with difficulty, but pushes bravely on without noticing those who fall by the way. It often happens that even in the narrow circle of the family, members are found as widely separated one from the other as this vanguard from the main army. All Russian authoresses of any reputation march in this vanguard. The retrogressive party can boast of no woman's name distinguished for thought or talent. Severin, the pseudonym of Mrs. Nadiejda Merder, Mrs. Olga Shapir, Mrs. Smirnova, and many others, have all published their works in the pages of progressive magazines. Vesseniev, the pseudonym of the late sister of Mrs. Zayontchkovsky, who was as sympathetic a writer and who wielded even a bolder pen, never contributed a line to the organs of the *statu quo.*

In other departments of literature I may cite the names of Mrs. Manasseina, author of many scientific articles on medicine and physiology, and of an excellent book on the physical training of children ; Mrs. Alexandra Efimenko, who has written many interesting essays on the Russian *mir* and the laws of custom among the peasants ; Miss Catharine Nekrasoff, who has published essays on Russian folklore ; Mrs. Vodovasoff, the author of a very important work for the young, "The Life of European Peoples " (*Jyzn evropeishih narodow*), and of many other children's books ; Mrs. Olga Novikoff, friend of Mme. Adam of the *Nouvelle Revue*, who has, besides magazine articles, printed a work on Russia ; and the late Mrs. Vernadsky, who published some twenty years ago a book on political economy, which is now forgotten, but was very honorably mentioned in its time. The tales of Ukrayna (Little Russia) by Marco Vovchok, the pseudonym of Mrs. Marie Markevitch, are a plea in favor of the political rights of the peasant classes, and are full of pathetic beauty. Some of them have been translated into French. I must not close this partial list of our female authors without mentioning one of great promise, but whose brilliant career, just opening, was suddenly cut short by death. Mrs. Sophy Bruloff was the daughter of Professor Kavelin, and in early childhood showed remarkable talents. Later she developed a strong taste for history, was sent abroad where she studied historical subjects with the greatest assiduity. She has written some very able essays on historical questions, and was making the preparatory notes for a great work on the epoch of Catharine II. when she died, at the early age of twenty-four.*

The Russian women's movement has one characteristic feature in which it differs from the similar movements elsewhere,—it is ever true to the ideas of progress. Whilst in other countries we sometimes see women striving for their own rights alone, for their own well-being, and in their eagerness to secure them, only too prone to make themselves the instrument of the church and conservatism, Russian women do not separate their cause from the great cause of human progress. The Jesuits in Europe have well understood, in their struggle for the preservation of old prejudices, what a powerful arm they should find in women equal and independent members of society and at the same time subservient to the will of the order. In England many Tories and high churchmen voted with Mr. John Stuart Mill in favor of women's suffrage. No retrogressive element in our society can count upon the aid of one woman battling for equality. The women who muster under that banner are quite satisfied with their dependent, inferior position, and pronounce as heresy every utterance for the emanci-

---

* Mommsen, in a note to me, referring to this female historian so full of promise, says : "The question is not, if women are capable or not, of high proficiency in every branch of learning, but if the average standing of man's and woman's capacity for these researches is equal or not, and this question cannot deal with exceptions." Montesquieu appears to answer the German historian when he says : "The powers [of the sexes] would be equal, if their education were too. Test them [women] in the talents which have not been enfeebled by the way they have been educated, and we will then see if we are so strong" (Lettres Persanes, lettre xxxviii.) L. Aimé Martin wrote, a half century ago : "It is in spite of our stupid systems of education that women have an idea, a mind and a soul."—T. S.

pation of their sex. Russian women who have risen to the consciousness of their right to knowledge and independence, consider these blessings as means with which to serve the people and improve the condition of their native land.

CARD & POCKET IN FRONT